RHINE RIVER CRUISE

The Ultimate Guide to Discover Attractive Castles, Locations Every Tourist Should Know and Explore

Rick A. Nicholas

1

Table of Contents

River cruises offer a fantastic way to explore the world's most picturesque waterways and immerse oneself in diverse cultures and landscapes. These cruises come in various styles and sizes, catering to different preferences and travel needs. Here are some common types of river cruise ships: 74

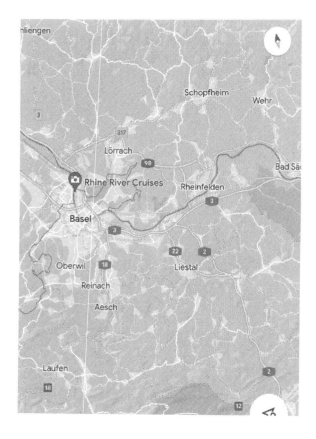

INTRODUCTION

In a world where rivers intertwined cultures and history, a curious traveler named Emma dreamt of exploring the renowned Rhine River, captivated by its allure and the tales whispered along its banks.

Excitement and anticipation filled Emma's heart as she stepped aboard a luxurious river cruise ship, ready to set sail on her grand adventure. However, amidst the anticipation, she also felt a tinge of uncertainty. With so much to see and experience along the Rhine's winding path, she didn't want to miss a single moment of its magic.

It was then that a fellow traveler, a wise old man named Mr. Thompson, noticed Emma's hesitation. With a knowing smile, he handed her a beautifully bound book - the Rhine River Cruising Travel Guide.

"Take this, young traveler," he said kindly, "This guide will be your compass, leading you through the wonders of the Rhine River. It holds the key to unlocking hidden gems, sharing the best times to visit each port, and offering insider tips that will ensure your journey is seamless and unforgettable."

Emma's eyes sparkled with gratitude as she flipped through the pages, discovering rich narratives, insightful recommendations, and practical advice. Throughout her voyage, the Rhine River Cruising Travel Guide proved to be a treasure trove of knowledge, enriching her journey and creating cherished memories that would forever be etched in her soul.

WELCOME TO THE RHINE RIVER!

Step aboard and prepare for an extraordinary journey along the majestic Rhine River, a waterway steeped in history, culture, and natural beauty. As you embark on this captivating adventure, our guide becomes your compass, leading you through the vast landscapes and captivating narratives that have unfolded along its banks for centuries.

The Rhine River, with its source nestled in the Swiss Alps and its final destination at the North Sea in the Netherlands, meanders through six countries – Switzerland, Liechtenstein, Austria, Germany, France, and the Netherlands. Along its winding course, you will encounter a tapestry of landscapes, from dramatic mountains to serene valleys, from ancient castles perched on hilltops to charming villages that seem straight out of a fairytale.

Our comprehensive Rhine River cruising travel guide is designed to be your trusted companion, providing you with valuable insights, practical tips, and exciting itineraries that will help you make the most of your journey. Whether you seek a relaxing retreat, a cultural adventure, or a gastronomic exploration, the Rhine River promises to fulfill your every desire.

So, sit back, relax, and let the gentle currents of the Rhine carry you along its storied waters. Allow yourself to be captivated by the ever-changing landscapes and the allure of the diverse cultures that call this river home. We are thrilled to accompany you on this remarkable voyage, and we hope that this guide will inspire you to create cherished memories as you discover the magic of the Rhine River. Bon voyage and welcome to the adventure of a lifetime!

Why Choose a Rhine River Cruise?

A Rhine River cruise offers a unique and unforgettable travel experience, enticing travelers from around the world to embark on this captivating journey. There are numerous reasons why choosing a Rhine River cruise is a decision you won't regret. Here are some of the compelling factors that make it a preferred choice for travelers:

Scenic Beauty: The Rhine River is renowned for its stunning and ever-changing landscapes. Cruising along its waters presents an enchanting panorama of rolling vineyards, ancient castles, charming villages, and picturesque valleys. From the breathtaking Rhine Gorge, often referred to as the "Romantic Rhine," to the serene landscapes of Switzerland, each bend in the river reveals a new postcard-perfect view.

Historic and Cultural Richness: As one of Europe's most historically significant waterways, the Rhine River boasts a wealth of cultural treasures and iconic landmarks. Along its banks, you'll encounter centuries-old castles, well-preserved medieval towns, and impressive cathedrals. The region's heritage is deeply intertwined with the river, and exploring its history is a journey back in time.

Convenient Exploration: A Rhine River cruise offers the convenience of exploring multiple destinations without the hassle of packing and unpacking at each stop. The cruise ship serves as a floating hotel, allowing you to wake up each morning in a new and exciting place, ready to embark on new adventures.

Enriching Shore Excursions: The well-planned shore excursions offered during a Rhine River cruise provide an opportunity to delve deeper into each destination. Knowledgeable guides lead you through iconic landmarks and lesser-known gems, offering valuable insights and stories that bring the history and culture of the region to life.

Culinary Delights: As the river passes through multiple countries, a Rhine River cruise presents a culinary feast for your taste buds. You'll savor the flavors of local cuisine, enjoy exquisite wines from renowned vineyards, and relish the delights of each region's gastronomic specialties.

Relaxation and Luxury: Onboard the cruise ship, you'll indulge in luxurious amenities and exceptional service. Unwind on the deck, enjoy the view from your comfortable cabin, or treat yourself to spa treatments, ensuring that relaxation is an essential part of your journey.

Flexibility and Choice: Rhine River cruises come in various durations and styles, catering to different preferences and interests. Whether you prefer an intimate boutique experience or a lively atmosphere with onboard entertainment, there's a cruise that aligns perfectly with your desires.

A Rhine River cruise is a captivating blend of history, culture, and scenic wonders, offering an experience that will stay with you long after the journey ends. It's a voyage that captures the heart and soul of Europe, making it an irresistible choice for travelers seeking a truly remarkable and enriching adventure.

Overview of the Rhine River Route

The Rhine River, one of Europe's most iconic waterways, weaves its way through six countries, offering an enchanting route that captivates travelers with its diverse landscapes, rich history, and cultural treasures. Spanning over 1,230 kilometers (765 miles) from its source in the Swiss Alps to its delta in the Netherlands, the Rhine River is a tapestry of experiences waiting to be explored.

The Rhine River route can be divided into three main sections, each with its distinct charm and highlights:

Upper Rhine: The journey begins in Switzerland, where the Rhine emerges as a pristine mountain stream. Navigating through Switzerland and a small section of Liechtenstein, this part of the river showcases picturesque alpine vistas, quaint villages, and charming towns like Basel. The Upper Rhine region is known for its serene beauty and opportunities for outdoor activities.

Middle Rhine: As the river winds its way into Germany, it enters the captivating Middle Rhine region, often referred to as the "Romantic Rhine." This stretch is famous for its dramatic landscapes, steep vineyard-covered hillsides, and legendary castles perched on rocky cliffs. The charming towns of Rüdesheim, Boppard, and Bacharach dot the route, transporting travelers to a fairy-tale world.

Lower Rhine: The final section of the Rhine River flows through Germany, forming the border with France, and eventually reaches the Netherlands. Here, the river widens, and lush landscapes with winding dikes and bustling ports take center stage. The vibrant cities of Cologne, Düsseldorf, and Amsterdam beckon with their cultural delights and historic landmarks.

Along the Rhine River route, travelers will encounter a blend of captivating history, captivating history, and a rich cultural heritage that has been shaped by the river's influence for centuries. From ancient Roman settlements to medieval castles and modern cities, the Rhine River offers an unparalleled journey through time.

PLANNING YOUR RHINE RIVER CRUISE

Best Time to Go

Choosing the perfect time for your Rhine River cruise can significantly enhance your experience, as each season presents a different side of this enchanting waterway. Here's a breakdown of the best times to go, each offering its own unique allure:

Spring (March to May): Springtime along the Rhine River brings a burst of colors as the landscape awakens from its winter slumber. Blooming flowers adorn the riverbanks, and the picturesque vineyards begin to sprout new leaves. The weather is mild, making it an ideal time for shore excursions and exploring charming towns. However, keep in mind that early spring may see higher water levels due to melting snow, affecting some cruise itineraries.

Summer (June to August): The summer months are peak season for Rhine River cruises. Warm and sunny weather sets the stage for idyllic cruising and delightful outdoor activities. The vineyards are lush and green, and riverside cafes buzz with life. But during this period, expect bigger crowds and more expensive prices. Advance booking is recommended to secure your preferred itinerary and accommodations.

Autumn (September to October): Fall, also known as the "golden season," is a favorite time for many travelers. The river valley is painted in hues of red, orange, and gold as the vineyards and forests change color. The weather remains pleasant, and tourist crowds start to dwindle, allowing for a more intimate experience. Additionally, wine enthusiasts can enjoy the harvest season with special wine-themed cruises and tastings.

Winter (November to February): Winter offers a different kind of charm along the Rhine River. The landscapes are serene, and some areas may be covered in a light dusting of snow. While cruising during this time is less common, it can be an excellent choice for those seeking a more tranquil and budget-friendly experience. Christmas markets in cities like Cologne and Strasbourg add a festive touch to the journey.

Ultimately, the best time to go on a Rhine River cruise depends on your preferences and what you wish to experience. Whether you prefer the vibrant ambiance of summer, the colorful scenery of fall, or the peacefulness of winter, each season holds its own magic along the Rhine River, promising an unforgettable journey through time and nature's wonders.

Duration of the Cruise

The duration of a Rhine River cruise can vary, offering travelers a range of options to suit their preferences and schedules. Typical Rhine River cruises can last anywhere from a few days to several weeks. Here are the most common durations available:

Short Cruises (4 to 7 days): Short cruises are perfect for those seeking a quick getaway or first-time river cruisers looking to experience the essence of the Rhine River. These cruises typically cover a specific section of the river, such as the Middle Rhine with its fairy-tale castles or the Upper Rhine through the stunning landscapes of Switzerland and Germany. Short cruises offer a taste of the region's culture, history, and scenic beauty while fitting easily into a week-long vacation.

Weeklong Cruises (7 to 10 days): Weeklong cruises provide a more comprehensive exploration of the Rhine River, allowing travelers to immerse themselves in the diverse landscapes and cultural highlights of the region. These cruises often cover more extensive sections of the river, passing through multiple countries and iconic cities. Weeklong cruises offer a balanced blend of leisurely cruising and immersive shore excursions, providing a well-rounded experience.

Extended Cruises (10+ days): For those seeking an in-depth exploration of the Rhine River and its neighboring waterways, extended cruises are an excellent choice. These cruises often combine the Rhine with other scenic rivers like the Danube or the Main, offering a grand European river adventure. Extended cruises allow travelers to uncover the hidden gems and off-the-beaten-path destinations that may not be included in shorter itineraries.

Whether you opt for a short, weeklong, or extended Rhine River cruise, each duration promises a remarkable journey, revealing the captivating beauty and cultural richness of this iconic waterway. Consider your available time, travel preferences, and desired level of exploration when choosing the duration that best suits your Rhine River adventure.

Choosing the Right Cruise Line

Selecting the perfect cruise line for your Rhine River adventure is a crucial step that can significantly influence your overall experience. Each cruise line offers its unique style, amenities, and itineraries, catering to different preferences and interests. Here are essential factors to consider when choosing the right cruise line for your Rhine River journey:

Cruise Style and Atmosphere: Determine the type of experience you desire. Some cruise lines offer a relaxed and intimate ambiance with a focus on cultural immersion, while others provide a more lively and entertaining atmosphere with onboard activities and shows. Consider whether you prefer a more casual or formal setting, and read reviews or testimonials from past travelers to get an idea of the cruise line's overall vibe.

Itinerary and Destinations: Review the cruise line's itineraries and the destinations they cover along the Rhine River. Some cruise lines may focus on specific regions or countries, while others offer more extensive journeys through multiple countries. Choose a cruise line that visits the destinations you are most interested in exploring.

Onboard Amenities: Assess the onboard amenities and facilities provided by each cruise line. Look for features that align with your preferences, such as spa services, fitness centers, swimming pools, gourmet dining options, and enrichment programs. Luxury cruise lines may offer more personalized services and exclusive experiences.

Shore Excursions: Investigate the shore excursions offered by each cruise line. Check if they include guided tours, cultural experiences, and active adventures. A variety of well-curated shore excursions can enhance your understanding and enjoyment of the destinations you visit.

Cabin Options: Consider the range of cabin categories available on each cruise line. Whether you prefer a cozy interior cabin or a luxurious suite with a private balcony, choose a cruise line that provides accommodation that matches your comfort level and budget.

Traveler Demographics: Some cruise lines cater more to families, while others focus on adult travelers or offer themed cruises for specific interests. Research the demographics of the cruise line's typical passengers to ensure it aligns with your preferences.

Reputation and Reviews: Read reviews from previous travelers to gain insight into their experiences with each cruise line. Reputable cruise lines with positive feedback and customer satisfaction are likely to provide a more enjoyable and rewarding journey.

By carefully considering these factors, you can make an informed decision and choose the right cruise line for your Rhine River adventure. A well-suited cruise line will complement your travel preferences, allowing you to savor the beauty, history, and cultural treasures of the Rhine River to the fullest.

Booking Your Cruise

Booking your Rhine River cruise is an exciting step towards embarking on a memorable journey through the heart of Europe. To ensure a seamless and enjoyable booking process, follow these essential tips:

Research and Compare: Begin by researching various cruise lines that offer Rhine River itineraries. Compare their offerings, including cruise duration, destinations, amenities, and inclusions. Pay attention to specific features that align with your preferences and interests.

Plan Ahead: Rhine River cruises, especially during peak seasons, can fill up quickly. To secure your preferred cabin and itinerary, consider booking well in advance, preferably several months before your desired travel date. Early booking may also offer benefits like discounted rates and cabin upgrades.

Travel Agents: Consider booking your Rhine River cruise through a reputable travel agent or cruise specialist. Experienced agents can provide valuable insights, help you find the best deals, and assist with any special requests or accommodations.

Flexible Dates: If your travel dates are flexible, check for availability across different departure dates. Certain departure dates may offer better rates or a more suitable itinerary, allowing you to tailor your journey to your liking.

Cabin Selection: Choose your cabin carefully, taking into account factors such as cabin location, size, and amenities. Balcony cabins offer stunning views and a private space to relax, while interior cabins may be more budget-friendly.

Inclusions and Add-ons: Be clear on what is included in the cruise package, such as meals, onboard activities, and some shore excursions. Additionally, inquire about optional add-ons or packages that may enhance your experience, such as premium beverage packages or specialty dining options.

Travel Insurance: Consider purchasing travel insurance to protect your investment and provide coverage for unforeseen circumstances, such as trip cancellations, medical emergencies, or lost luggage.

Payment and Policies: Review the cruise line's payment and cancellation policies to understand any deposit requirements and deadlines for final payments. Familiarize yourself with cancellation fees and refund policies in case your plans change.

Document Preparation: Ensure you have all necessary travel documents, such as passports and visas, well in advance of your departure date.

Special Requests: If you have any special dietary preferences, medical needs, or mobility requirements, inform the cruise line or your travel agent during the booking process. They'll try their best to fulfill your requests.

Booking your Rhine River cruise with careful consideration and preparation will set the stage for an exceptional journey. As you secure your reservation, anticipation will build, knowing that soon you'll be embarking on a voyage filled with scenic beauty, cultural treasures, and cherished memories along the storied banks of the Rhine River.

Preparing for the Trip

Preparing for your Rhine River cruise is an essential step in ensuring a smooth and enjoyable journey. Here are some key aspects to consider as you get ready for your adventure:

Travel Documentation: Check and ensure that you have all the necessary travel documents, including a valid passport with at least six months' validity beyond your travel dates. Depending on your nationality and the countries you'll be visiting, you may also need visas or other travel permits.

Health and Vaccinations: Consult with your healthcare provider to ensure you are up-to-date on routine vaccinations and discuss any additional vaccinations or health precautions recommended for the regions you'll be visiting. Consider travel insurance that covers medical emergencies and travel disruptions.

Packing Essentials: Pack appropriate clothing for the season and weather during your cruise. Comfortable walking shoes, layers for varying temperatures, and rain gear are essential. Don't forget essentials like chargers, adapters, and any medications you may need.

Currency and Payments: Familiarize yourself with the currency used in the countries along the Rhine River route and consider carrying some local currency for small expenses. Notify your bank of your travel plans to avoid any issues with credit card usage abroad.

Shore Excursions: Review the shore excursions offered by your cruise line and consider pre-booking any excursions that interest you. This will ensure you secure a spot and allow you to plan your daily activities more efficiently.

Travel Itinerary: Make a copy of your travel itinerary, including flight details, cruise reservations, and any other pre- or post-cruise arrangements you may have made. Share this information with a trusted friend or family member for added safety.

Travel Insurance: Purchase comprehensive travel insurance that covers trip cancellations, medical emergencies, baggage loss, and other unforeseen events. Travel insurance provides peace of mind during your journey.

Language and Culture: Familiarize yourself with common phrases and greetings in the languages spoken along the Rhine River, such as German and French. Your encounters with locals will benefit from learning a few fundamental terms.

Cruise Line Information: Review the details provided by your cruise line, including embarkation instructions, onboard services, and dress codes. Familiarize yourself with the ship's layout and amenities to settle in more quickly.

Informing Loved Ones: Inform family or friends of your travel plans, including your cruise itinerary and contact information. Staying connected while traveling ensures peace of mind for both you and your loved ones.

By taking these preparatory steps, you'll be well-equipped for an enriching and stress-free Rhine River cruise experience.

Travel Insurance and Health Considerations

When preparing for your Rhine River cruise, two critical aspects to prioritize are travel insurance and health considerations. These factors ensure your safety, well-being, and peace of mind throughout your journey.

Travel Insurance

Purchasing comprehensive travel insurance is highly recommended for any international trip, including a Rhine River cruise. Travel insurance provides financial protection against unexpected events that could disrupt or impact your travel plans. Here are some essential aspects to consider when selecting travel insurance:

Trip Cancellation and Interruption: Travel insurance can reimburse you for non-refundable trip costs if you have to cancel or interrupt your cruise due to covered reasons such as illness, injury, or unforeseen circumstances.

Medical Coverage: Ensure that your travel insurance includes adequate medical coverage for emergencies and accidents that may occur during your trip. This should cover medical expenses, hospitalization, and emergency medical evacuation if necessary.

Baggage and Personal Belongings: Travel insurance can provide compensation in case your luggage is lost, stolen, or damaged during your journey. It also covers personal belongings like cameras, electronics, and valuable items.

Travel Delays and Missed Connections: In the event of flight delays or missed connections, travel insurance can cover additional expenses for accommodations, meals, and transportation.

Emergency Assistance: Look for travel insurance that offers 24/7 emergency assistance services. This includes access to a helpline for medical advice, travel-related emergencies, and support during unforeseen situations.

Health Considerations

Before embarking on your Rhine River cruise, consider these health considerations to ensure a safe and enjoyable journey:

Vaccinations: Check with your healthcare provider to ensure you are up-to-date on routine vaccinations. Additionally, inquire about any recommended or required vaccinations for the countries you'll be visiting along the Rhine River.

Medications: Pack all necessary medications in their original packaging, and carry a copy of your prescriptions. If you require specific medications during your cruise, ensure you have an adequate supply.

Medical Conditions: If you have any pre-existing medical conditions, inform your travel insurance provider, and consider obtaining a letter from your healthcare provider describing your condition and treatment plan.

Hydration and Health: Drink plenty of water during your cruise, as staying hydrated is essential, especially during warmer weather or active shore excursions. Follow health guidelines to protect against common travel-related illnesses.

Medical Facilities: Familiarize yourself with the locations of medical facilities and pharmacies in the cities you'll be visiting. Note the emergency number for each country (e.g., 112 in most European countries) in case of urgent medical assistance.

By prioritizing travel insurance and health considerations, you'll ensure a secure and worry-free Rhine River cruise experience.

RHINE RIVER DESTINATIONS

Amsterdam, Netherlands

Amsterdam, the capital city of the Netherlands, is a vibrant and captivating destination that attracts millions of visitors each year. Known for its picturesque canals, rich history, artistic heritage, and diverse cultural scene, Amsterdam offers a unique and enchanting experience for travelers.

Canals and Architecture

One of Amsterdam's most iconic features is its intricate canal system, earning it the nickname "Venice of the North." The Canal Ring, a UNESCO World Heritage site, showcases stunning 17th-century architecture, picturesque bridges, and charming canal houses with gabled facades. A canal cruise is a must-do activity to appreciate the city's beauty from the water.

Cultural Delights

Amsterdam is steeped in cultural treasures and world-class museums. The Rijksmuseum houses an impressive collection of Dutch Golden Age art, including masterpieces by Rembrandt and Vermeer. The Van Gogh Museum celebrates the life and works of Vincent van Gogh, while the Anne Frank House offers a poignant glimpse into the life of Anne Frank during World War II.

Art and Creativity

The city's creative spirit is evident in its many art galleries, cutting-edge design boutiques, and vibrant street art scene. Visitors can explore the Jordaan neighborhood, known for its artistic flair, or visit contemporary art spaces like the Stedelijk Museum and the EYE Film Institute.

Historic Landmarks

Amsterdam boasts historic landmarks that tell the story of its past. The Royal Palace on Dam Square, the Westerkerk church with its famous bell tower, and the Oude Kerk, Amsterdam's oldest building, are just a few of the city's architectural treasures.

Tolerance and Diversity

Amsterdam is known for its progressive and inclusive culture. It embraces diversity and is home to various ethnic neighborhoods, making it a melting pot of cultures and cuisines. The city's open-minded approach is evident in its LGBTQ+ friendly establishments, earning it a reputation as one of the most LGBTQ+ friendly cities in the world.

Culinary Delights

Amsterdam offers a vibrant culinary scene with restaurants and eateries serving a wide array of cuisines from around the world. Don't miss the opportunity to savor traditional Dutch dishes like stroopwafels, bitterballen, and herring from street-side vendors.

Bicycling Capital

Bicycling is a way of life in Amsterdam, and cycling through the city's bike-friendly streets is a popular and enjoyable way to explore. Rent a bike and pedal along the canals and leafy parks, immersing yourself in the local lifestyle.

Amsterdam's unique blend of history, culture, and modernity creates an alluring destination that never fails to captivate its visitors. Whether you're strolling along the canals, admiring masterpieces at world-class museums, or simply soaking up the vibrant atmosphere, Amsterdam promises an unforgettable and enriching experience for every traveler.

Top Attractions in Amsterdam

Amsterdam, the enchanting capital of the Netherlands, is teeming with captivating attractions that cater to a diverse range of interests. From its iconic canals to its world-class museums, the city offers an array of experiences that make it a must-visit destination. Here are some of the top attractions to explore in Amsterdam:

Rijksmuseum: Housing an extensive collection of Dutch Golden Age art, the Rijksmuseum is a treasure trove of masterpieces by renowned artists such as Rembrandt, Vermeer, and Hals. Visitors can immerse themselves in the rich history of Dutch art and culture as they admire its vast collection.

Van Gogh Museum: Dedicated to the life and works of the iconic artist Vincent van Gogh, this museum houses the largest collection of Van Gogh's paintings in the world. It offers a fascinating journey through the artist's creative evolution and personal struggles.

Anne Frank House: A poignant reminder of the Holocaust, the Anne Frank House is where Anne Frank and her family hid from the Nazis during World War II. The museum offers a moving experience as visitors learn about Anne's life through her diary and the secret annex where she lived.

Canal Cruises: Exploring Amsterdam's canals is an absolute must. Take a leisurely canal cruise to admire the city's picturesque canal houses, charming bridges, and historic landmarks from a unique perspective.

Jordaan District: Wander through the bohemian neighborhood of Jordaan, known for its artistic ambiance, quaint cafes, and boutique shops. It's a delightful area to soak in Amsterdam's creative spirit and local culture.

Vondelpark: Amsterdam's most famous park, Vondelpark, is a lush oasis perfect for picnics, leisurely strolls, or simply unwinding amidst nature. It's a beloved spot for both locals and visitors alike.

Heineken Experience: Beer enthusiasts will enjoy the interactive Heineken Experience, where they can learn about the brewing process, the brand's history, and even sample some freshly brewed beer.

Dam Square: At the heart of Amsterdam, Dam Square is a bustling hub surrounded by significant landmarks such as the Royal Palace and the National Monument. It's an ideal starting point for exploring the city's historic center.

Red Light District: The Red Light District is known for its vibrant nightlife and distinctive red-lit windows. While it may not be everyone's cup of tea, it remains a curious attraction, offering insight into Amsterdam's liberal approach to certain industries.

Albert Cuyp Market: Amsterdam's most famous street market, Albert Cuyp Market, is a treasure trove of food, clothing, souvenirs, and more. It's an excellent place to sample local delicacies and shop for unique finds.

From cultural landmarks and artistic masterpieces to leisurely strolls along the canals, Amsterdam's top attractions promise an enriching and unforgettable experience.

Canal Cruises and Sightseeing in Amsterdam

Amsterdam's canal cruises are an essential and delightful way to experience the city's enchanting beauty and rich history. The intricate network of canals, with their elegant bridges and picturesque canal houses, offers a unique and charming backdrop for exploring Amsterdam's top attractions. Here's why canal cruises are a must-do activity and some of the sights you can expect to see:

Why Choose Canal Cruises

Unparalleled Perspectives: Canal cruises provide unparalleled perspectives of Amsterdam's iconic landmarks and architectural gems. From the water, you'll gain a new appreciation for the city's layout and its harmonious blend of historical and modern structures.

Leisurely Exploration: Cruising along the canals is a leisurely and relaxing way to explore the city. As you glide through the waterways, you'll be able to take in the sights at a leisurely pace, allowing you to savor the ambiance and beauty of each location.

Guided Narration: Many canal cruises offer guided narrations in multiple languages, providing insightful commentary about the history, culture, and significance of the sights you pass by. This enhances your understanding of Amsterdam's heritage and adds depth to your experience.

Scenic Photo Opportunities: The photo opportunities from a canal cruise are exceptional. Capture postcard-perfect shots of historic canal houses, charming bridges, and idyllic vistas that will become cherished memories of your journey.

Top Sights on Canal Cruises

Canal Ring: The Canal Ring, a UNESCO World Heritage site, is a top sight on any canal cruise. The iconic canal houses with their gabled facades, historic bridges, and tree-lined waterways create a dreamy and romantic ambiance.

Anne Frank House: From the water, you'll see the front of the Anne Frank House, offering a unique perspective of this poignant landmark. Note that the entrance to the museum is on land and requires a separate visit.

Westerkerk Church: Cruise past the majestic Westerkerk church and its famous bell tower, the Westertoren. This landmark has historical significance and is associated with Dutch painter Rembrandt, who was buried nearby.

Skinny Bridge (Magere Brug): Admire the charming Skinny Bridge, a double-leaf, traditional Dutch drawbridge that spans the Amstel River. It's especially magical when illuminated at night.

Seven Bridges (Zevenbruggetjes): The Seven Bridges is a series of seven small bridges in the Jordaan neighborhood, forming an iconic Amsterdam scene. It's particularly picturesque when the canal is adorned with colorful flowers.

Amstel River: Cruise along the scenic Amstel River, where you can enjoy panoramic views of Amsterdam's riverside architecture and lively waterfront terraces.

Canal cruises and sightseeing in Amsterdam offer a captivating and enchanting experience, allowing you to immerse yourself in the city's charm and allure.

Cultural Highlights

Amsterdam's rich cultural heritage and diverse artistic scene make it a thriving hub of creativity and exploration. From world-class museums to vibrant neighborhoods, the city offers a wealth of cultural highlights that captivate travelers from around the globe. Here are some of the top cultural attractions that you won't want to miss during your visit to Amsterdam:

Rijksmuseum: The Rijksmuseum is an absolute treasure trove of Dutch Golden Age art and history. With an extensive collection that includes masterpieces by Rembrandt, Vermeer, and Hals, the museum offers a captivating journey through the country's artistic legacy and cultural heritage.

Van Gogh Museum: Dedicated to the iconic artist Vincent van Gogh, this museum houses the largest collection of Van Gogh's paintings in the world. It provides a profound insight into Van Gogh's life, creative process, and artistic evolution, making it a must-visit for art enthusiasts.

Anne Frank House: A significant cultural landmark, the Anne Frank House offers a moving and poignant experience as visitors learn about Anne Frank's life and the harrowing experiences of those in hiding during World War II. The museum provides a powerful reminder of the importance of tolerance and understanding.

Concertgebouw: As one of the world's most renowned concert halls, the Concertgebouw hosts classical concerts by top orchestras and musicians. Its exceptional acoustics and elegant architecture make it a cultural gem for music lovers.

Jordaan Neighborhood: Stroll through the charming Jordaan neighborhood, known for its artistic flair and lively cultural scene. Here, you'll find art galleries, design boutiques, cozy cafes, and local markets that reflect the city's creative spirit.

Stedelijk Museum: Amsterdam's premier museum of modern and contemporary art, the Stedelijk Museum showcases works by renowned artists such as Mondrian, Picasso, and Warhol. It's a hub of creativity and innovation, with changing exhibitions that reflect contemporary art movements.

Royal Palace Amsterdam: Originally built as a city hall during the Dutch Golden Age, the Royal Palace is a symbol of Amsterdam's history and regal heritage. Visitors can explore its opulent interiors and grand halls.

De Pijp District: De Pijp is a diverse and vibrant neighborhood, known for its multicultural atmosphere, artistic community, and bustling street markets. The Albert Cuyp Market is a fantastic place to experience the local culture and cuisine.

EYE Film Institute: Film enthusiasts will enjoy a visit to the EYE Film Institute, where the world of cinema comes alive through screenings, exhibitions, and interactive displays. The futuristic architecture of the building itself is a sight to behold.

National Maritime Museum: For a glimpse into the Netherlands' maritime history, visit the National Maritime Museum. It houses a vast collection of maritime artifacts, models, and interactive exhibits that showcase the nation's seafaring legacy.

Amsterdam's cultural highlights offer an enriching experience that celebrates the city's art, history, and creative spirit.

Donning and Entertainment

Amsterdam's vibrant culinary scene and lively entertainment options offer a delightful fusion of flavors and experiences that cater to diverse tastes and preferences. From traditional Dutch delicacies to international cuisine and a range of entertainment venues, the city ensures a memorable dining and entertainment experience for every visitor. Here are some highlights to indulge in during your stay:

Dining

Dutch Cuisine: Sample authentic Dutch dishes like stroopwafels (thin caramel-filled waffles), bitterballen (deep-fried meatballs), and poffertjes (mini pancakes) from local street vendors or traditional eateries.

Indonesian Restaurants: Amsterdam's historical ties with Indonesia have resulted in a rich Indonesian culinary influence. Try rijsttafel (a selection of small Indonesian dishes) for a delectable and flavorful feast.

Dutch Cheese: Visit the city's cheese shops to savor an array of delicious Dutch cheeses like Gouda, Edam, and Leerdammer. Many markets offer cheese tastings and opportunities to buy souvenirs to take home.

Culinary Diversity: Explore the multicultural neighborhoods of Amsterdam, such as De Pijp or Oud-West, where you'll find a wide variety of international cuisines, from Thai and Surinamese to Ethiopian and Lebanese.

Michelin-Starred Restaurants: For a refined and gourmet experience, dine at one of Amsterdam's Michelin-starred restaurants, which showcase innovative and artistic culinary creations.

Brown Cafes: Visit traditional Dutch brown cafes, cozy and historic pubs, to enjoy a relaxed atmosphere while sipping on local beers or trying a jenever (Dutch gin).

Food Markets: Immerse yourself in the bustling food markets, such as Albert Cuyp Market or Foodhallen, where you can taste a diverse range of international street food and local specialties.

Entertainment

Concerts and Music Venues: Amsterdam boasts a lively music scene with concerts and performances taking place in venues like the Concertgebouw, Paradiso, and Melkweg. Enjoy anything from classical concerts to contemporary music gigs.

Nightlife in Leidseplein and Rembrandtplein: Experience Amsterdam's nightlife in the vibrant areas of Leidseplein and Rembrandtplein, where you'll find a plethora of bars, clubs, and live music venues.

Theatres and Performance Art: Catch a theatrical production, comedy show, or dance performance at one of the city's theatres, such as the Royal Theater Carré or the Stadsschouwburg.

Café Culture: Amsterdam's cafe culture is an integral part of its entertainment scene. Relax in cozy cafes and enjoy conversations with friends, people-watching, or reading a book.

Canal Cruises by Night: Experience the city's enchanting ambiance on a nighttime canal cruise, where you'll see Amsterdam's landmarks beautifully illuminated.

Amsterdam ArenA: If you're a sports enthusiast, consider attending a football match or concert at the Amsterdam ArenA, home to AFC Ajax football club.

Amsterdam's dining and entertainment scene is as diverse as its culture. Whether you're seeking a culinary adventure, a night of live music, or a leisurely evening by the canals, the city promises an array of options to suit your preferences and create lasting memories of your Amsterdam experience.

Cologne, Germany

Cologne, or Köln in German, is a vibrant city located along the banks of the Rhine River in western Germany. Known for its rich history, stunning architecture, and lively cultural scene, Cologne is a captivating destination that offers a perfect blend of tradition and modernity. Here are some of this lovely city's highlights:

Cologne Cathedral (Kölner Dom)

Cologne's most famous landmark and a UNESCO World Heritage site, the Cologne Cathedral is an awe-inspiring masterpiece of Gothic architecture. With its soaring twin spires and intricate façade, the cathedral dominates the city's skyline. Inside, visitors can admire stunning stained glass windows and the Shrine of the Three Kings, said to contain relics of the biblical Magi.

Old Town (Altstadt)

The Old Town of Cologne is a charming area with narrow cobblestone streets, colorful houses, and lively squares. It is home to numerous historic buildings, museums, and churches, making it a delightful place to wander and soak in the city's ambiance. Don't miss the picturesque Alter Markt and Heumarkt squares, where you can enjoy local food and drinks in traditional pubs.

Hohenzollern Bridge (Hohenzollernbrücke)

The Hohenzollern Bridge is a famous pedestrian and railway bridge that spans the Rhine River. It is adorned with thousands of love locks placed by couples as a symbol of their eternal love. The bridge also offers stunning views of the cathedral and the river, making it a popular spot for romantic walks and photographs.

Ludwig Museum (Museum Ludwig)
Art enthusiasts will appreciate a visit to the Ludwig Museum, which houses an impressive collection of modern and contemporary art. It is renowned for its significant collection of works by artists such as Pablo Picasso, Andy Warhol, and Roy Lichtenstein. The museum also showcases a remarkable selection of pop art and abstract art.

Rheinauhafen
Rheinauhafen is a modern waterfront district characterized by its unique architecture and vibrant atmosphere. The area features sleek office buildings, upscale apartments, and stylish restaurants and bars. The Kranhäuser, three distinctive crane-shaped buildings, are some of the most iconic structures in this rejuvenated district.

Cologne Chocolate Museum (Schokoladenmuseum)
Chocolate lovers will find their paradise at the Cologne Chocolate Museum, where they can learn about the history of chocolate and witness the chocolate-making process. The museum offers interactive exhibits, a cocoa tree greenhouse, and plenty of opportunities to indulge in sweet treats.

Cologne Cable Car (Kölner Seilbahn)

For panoramic views of the city and the Rhine River, take a ride on the Cologne Cable Car. The cable car spans the river between the Zoobrücke and the Rheinpark, offering a thrilling and unique perspective of Cologne.

Cologne is a city with a rich cultural heritage, a vibrant urban life, and an undeniable charm. Whether you're exploring its historical landmarks, admiring its stunning architecture, or indulging in its cultural offerings, Cologne promises an unforgettable and rewarding experience for every traveler.

The Iconic Cologne Cathedral

Standing majestically on the banks of the Rhine River, the Cologne Cathedral, or Kölner Dom in German, is an awe-inspiring masterpiece of Gothic architecture and an iconic symbol of the city of Cologne, Germany. With its soaring twin spires and intricate façade, the cathedral is a testament to human creativity, determination, and faith.

Construction of the Cologne Cathedral began in 1248, but it took over six centuries to complete this magnificent structure. It is considered one of the largest cathedrals in Europe and a UNESCO World Heritage site. The cathedral's impressive dimensions include a length of 144 meters (472 feet), a width of 86 meters (282 feet), and spires that reach a height of 157 meters (515 feet).

The exterior of the cathedral is adorned with countless stone sculptures, intricate details, and ornate decorations. The façade's focal point is the grand West Portal, featuring statues of saints, angels, and biblical figures. The cathedral's most revered relic, the Shrine of the Three Kings (Dreikönigsschrein), is housed inside. This golden shrine is said to contain the remains of the Three Wise Men who visited the baby Jesus, making it an essential pilgrimage site for Christians.

Visitors to the Cologne Cathedral can marvel at its stunning stained glass windows, which date back to various periods and depict biblical scenes and saints. One of the highlights is the South Transept window, known as the "Window of the Last Judgment," which is a masterpiece of medieval glass art.

Ascending to the top of the cathedral's spires offers a breathtaking panorama of Cologne and its surroundings. The climb, comprising 533 steps, rewards visitors with awe-inspiring views and a closer look at the intricate stonework.

Throughout its history, the Cologne Cathedral has faced challenges, including damages during World War II bombings. However, thanks to extensive restoration efforts, the cathedral has been meticulously preserved to continue inspiring awe and wonder in generations of visitors.

As one of Germany's most visited landmarks, the Cologne Cathedral holds not only immense religious significance but also cultural and architectural importance. Its towering presence and intricate design reflect the resilience and artistry of humankind, making it a cherished symbol of Cologne and a cherished destination for travelers from around the world.

Historic Old Town

Stepping into the historic Old Town (Altstadt) of Cologne is like embarking on a journey back in time. This charming neighborhood, nestled along the western banks of the Rhine River, is a living testament to the city's rich history and cultural heritage. With its narrow cobblestone streets, medieval buildings, and lively squares, the Old

Town is a captivating district that offers a delightful blend of tradition, art, and modernity.

Highlights of the Historic Old Town
Cologne Cathedral (Kölner Dom): The crown jewel of the Old Town is undoubtedly the Cologne Cathedral, a towering Gothic masterpiece that looms over the city's skyline. As one of the most significant cathedrals in Europe, it draws visitors from far and wide with its breathtaking architecture and spiritual significance.

Alter Markt: The lively heart of the Old Town, Alter Markt is a picturesque square surrounded by colorful historical buildings. It exudes a welcoming atmosphere and is home to traditional pubs and restaurants, making it an excellent spot to sample local delicacies and immerse yourself in Cologne's vibrant culture.

Heumarkt: Just a short stroll from Alter Markt, Heumarkt is another bustling square known for its lively nightlife and festive events. This vibrant area is a favorite among locals and visitors alike, especially during the city's annual carnival celebrations.

Great St. Martin Church (Groß St. Martin): This Romanesque church with its characteristic twin towers is another prominent landmark in the Old Town. It stands near the riverbank, adding to the picturesque beauty of the area.

Historic Houses and Museums: The Old Town is peppered with historic houses, some of which have been converted into museums, art galleries, and cultural centers. Visiting these establishments offers glimpses into Cologne's past and its vibrant artistic scene.

Rathaus (City Hall): The Rathaus is a splendid building that showcases the city's architectural elegance. It is a blend of different styles, with its Renaissance-style façade and medieval foundations. Guided tours are available for those interested in delving into the history and inner workings of the city's administration.

Cologne's Old Town is not just a collection of historical sites; it's a lively and dynamic district that comes to life with local events, markets, and festivals. Whether you're exploring its cultural landmarks, enjoying a leisurely stroll along the Rhine promenade, or savoring the authentic charm of its cafes and shops, the Historic Old Town of Cologne promises an enriching and unforgettable experience for every visitor.

Local Cuisine and Beer

Cologne, a city rich in culinary traditions and brewing heritage, offers a delightful array of local cuisine and beer that reflect the region's distinct flavors and culture. From hearty dishes that warm the soul to refreshing brews that quench the thirst, experiencing the local food and drink scene is an essential part of any visit to Cologne.

Local Cuisine

Kölsch: Cologne's iconic beer, Kölsch, is not just a beverage but a way of life for locals. Served in small, slender glasses, this light and crisp beer is best enjoyed at one of the city's traditional breweries or beer halls. The beer is typically served with a Kölschstange, a beer coaster that helps keep track of how many you've had.

Himmel un Ääd: A quintessential Cologne dish, Himmel un Ääd (Heaven and Earth) combines mashed potatoes with applesauce and blood sausage. The combination of sweet and savory flavors is a unique and comforting culinary experience.

Rheinischer Sauerbraten: This traditional pot roast is marinated in a mix of vinegar, water, and spices, giving it a distinctive sour taste. Served with red cabbage and potato dumplings, Rheinischer Sauerbraten is a hearty and flavorful dish that showcases Cologne's regional cooking style.

Reibekuchen: These savory potato pancakes are a popular street food snack in Cologne. Served hot and crispy, they are often accompanied by applesauce or a dollop of sour cream.

Halver Hahn: Despite its name ("half a rooster" in English), Halver Hahn is not a chicken dish. Instead, it's an open-faced sandwich made with rye bread, butter, gouda cheese, and mustard.

Rievkooche: Another variation of potato pancakes, Rievkooche are thicker and fluffier. They are sometimes served with bacon or sour cream for added indulgence.

Local Beer

As mentioned earlier, Kölsch is the city's signature beer and an integral part of Cologne's culture. Brewed according to strict regulations, Kölsch is light, refreshing, and best enjoyed fresh from the tap.

Altbier: While Kölsch is the dominant beer style in Cologne, you can also find Altbier, a dark, top-fermented beer that originates from the neighboring city of Düsseldorf. Some bars and pubs in Cologne offer Altbier as an alternative to Kölsch.

Local Craft Breweries: In recent years, the craft beer scene has also gained momentum in Cologne, with several local breweries producing innovative and unique brews. These craft beers often feature creative flavors and styles, offering a modern twist on traditional brewing.

Cologne's local cuisine and beer are integral to the city's identity and culture. Whether you're savoring traditional dishes in cozy taverns or sampling the city's renowned Kölsch at a bustling beer hall, embracing the local food and drink scene is an excellent way to immerse yourself in the heart and soul of Cologne. Prost! (Cheers!)

Strasbourg, France

Nestled near the border of Germany and France, Strasbourg is a captivating city that boasts a unique blend of both cultures. This capital of the Alsace region is renowned for its picturesque canals, half-timbered houses, and enchanting neighborhoods, making it a true gem in the heart of Europe. With its rich history, distinct architecture, and vibrant atmosphere, Strasbourg offers an unforgettable experience for travelers.

Historic Center (Grande Île)

Strasbourg's historic center, known as the Grande Île, is a UNESCO World Heritage site and a treasure trove of architectural marvels. Here, visitors can wander through cobblestone streets, marvel at well-preserved medieval buildings, and explore iconic landmarks such as the Strasbourg Cathedral (Cathédrale Notre-Dame) with its intricate façade and towering spire.

Petite France

Petite France is a charming neighborhood located on the Grande Île, famous for its quaint half-timbered houses and idyllic canals. This area exudes a fairytale-like ambiance, and it is a delightful place to stroll along the waterways, visit artisan shops, and enjoy Alsatian cuisine in traditional restaurants.

European Quarter

Strasbourg is not only known for its historical significance but also as the official seat of several European institutions. The European Quarter houses the European Parliament, the Council of Europe, and the European Court of Human Rights. Visitors can learn about the European Union's work through guided tours and exhibitions.

Museums and Cultural Attractions

Strasbourg's cultural offerings are diverse and plentiful. The Strasbourg Museum of Fine Arts (Musée des Beaux-Arts) showcases an extensive collection of European artwork, while the Alsatian Museum (Musée Alsacien) offers insights into the region's unique heritage. Additionally, the

Strasbourg Museum of Modern and Contemporary Art (Musée d'Art Moderne et Contemporain) features works by modern artists.

Boat Tours and Canals

Exploring Strasbourg's canals is a must-do activity. Taking a boat tour allows visitors to admire the city's stunning architecture, historic bridges, and the charming neighborhoods that line the waterways. Boat tours provide an enchanting perspective of Strasbourg's beauty.

Christmas Markets

Strasbourg is famous for hosting one of Europe's oldest and most charming Christmas markets. The festive atmosphere, twinkling lights, and aroma of mulled wine and gingerbread fill the air during the Advent season, making it a magical destination for Christmas enthusiasts.

Alsatian Cuisine

Strasbourg's culinary scene is a gastronomic delight, with a focus on Alsatian cuisine. Savor traditional dishes like choucroute garnie (sauerkraut with sausages and meats), flammekueche (thin savory tart), and baeckeoffe (meat and vegetable casserole). Pair these delectable meals with local wines from the Alsace region.

Strasbourg, with its blend of French and German influences, offers a captivating journey through history, culture, and stunning architecture. Whether you're exploring its well-preserved historic center, cruising its scenic canals, or savoring the flavors of Alsatian cuisine, Strasbourg promises an enriching and unforgettable experience for every traveler.

Strasbourg Cathedral and La Petite France

Strasbourg Cathedral (Cathédrale Notre-Dame) and La Petite France are two of the most enchanting and iconic attractions in Strasbourg, France. These landmarks epitomize the city's rich history, architectural splendor, and undeniable charm, attracting visitors from around the world.

Strasbourg Cathedral (Cathédrale Notre-Dame)

As the centerpiece of Strasbourg's historic center, Strasbourg Cathedral is an awe-inspiring masterpiece of Gothic architecture. Its soaring spire, standing at 142 meters (466 feet) tall, dominated the city's skyline for centuries. The cathedral's construction began in 1176 and continued for centuries, resulting in a stunning fusion of architectural styles.

The cathedral's intricate façade is adorned with countless sculptures and ornate details, including the famous Astronomical Clock, a marvel of medieval engineering and artistry. Inside, visitors are greeted by the resplendent interior, featuring breathtaking stained glass windows that bathe the cathedral in a kaleidoscope of colors. The highlight is the stunning rose window on the west side, which is a masterpiece of Gothic stained glass art.

Ascending the cathedral's tower is a rewarding experience, offering panoramic views of Strasbourg and the surrounding Alsace countryside. The climb, though challenging, is well worth the effort for the unparalleled vistas that await at the top.

La Petite France
Located on the Grande Île, Strasbourg's historic island, La Petite France is a picturesque neighborhood characterized by its charming half-timbered houses, cobbled streets, and scenic canals. This idyllic district is a postcard-perfect destination that captures the essence of Strasbourg's medieval heritage.

La Petite France was once a bustling commercial area, home to millers, tanners, and fishermen. Today, the neighborhood exudes a fairytale-like ambiance, inviting visitors to wander its narrow alleys and admire the beautifully preserved buildings. The quaint houses with colorful flower boxes are reflected in the calm waters of the canals, creating a picture of timeless beauty.

The district is intersected by the River Ill, and its canals are spanned by charming stone bridges that add to the romantic charm of La Petite France. The name "Petite France" is said to be derived from the 16th-century Hospice of the Syphilitic, which was formerly known as "Franzosenkrankheit" (French Disease).

La Petite France is also known for its delightful restaurants and cafes, offering the perfect setting to indulge in Alsatian cuisine while soaking up the enchanting atmosphere.

Strasbourg Cathedral and La Petite France represent the soul of the city, embodying its historical significance and architectural beauty. Together, these landmarks offer a captivating journey through time, art, and culture, leaving visitors with cherished memories of the unique allure of Strasbourg, France.

Alsatian Culture and Gastronomy

The Alsatian region, nestled between the Vosges Mountains and the Rhine River in eastern France, boasts a vibrant and unique culture that reflects its rich history and diverse influences. The Alsatian culture is a captivating blend of French and German traditions, creating a tapestry of customs, architecture, and gastronomy that sets it apart from the rest of France.

Architecture and Heritage

Alsatian architecture is characterized by charming half-timbered houses, flower-filled windows, and colorful facades. The region's picturesque villages, such as Riquewihr and Eguisheim, are like stepping into a fairytale with their well-preserved medieval buildings and winding cobblestone streets. The mix of French and German influences is evident in the architecture, reflecting the area's history of changing hands between the two countries over the centuries.

Language and Dialects

Alsatian, a unique dialect with both German and French roots, is still spoken by some locals, especially in rural areas. While French is the official language, the Alsatian dialect adds a distinct linguistic aspect to the region's cultural identity.

Traditions and Festivals

Alsatians are proud of their customs and traditions, which are celebrated through various festivals and events throughout the year. The region is renowned for its festive Christmas markets, where the streets come alive with lights, decorations, and delicious treats, creating a magical holiday atmosphere. The Alsatian carnival, held in the spring, is another lively event, with colorful parades, traditional costumes, and plenty of music and dancing.

Gastronomy

Alsatian cuisine is a gastronomic delight, combining French finesse with hearty German flavors. The region's fertile lands and vineyards provide an abundance of fresh produce and wine, which are integral to Alsatian dishes. Some of the culinary highlights of Alsatian gastronomy include:

Choucroute Garnie: A signature Alsatian dish, choucroute garnie is a hearty platter of sauerkraut cooked with various meats, such as sausages, pork, and sometimes even fish or duck. It's a delectable combination of flavors and textures, served with mustard and potatoes.

Flammekueche (Tarte Flambée): Similar to a thin-crust pizza, flammekueche is a savory tart topped with crème fraîche, onions, and bacon. It's a popular and satisfying dish enjoyed by both locals and visitors.

Baeckeoffe: This traditional casserole dish consists of marinated meats (beef, pork, and lamb) layered with potatoes, onions, and carrots, then slow-cooked with wine and seasonings. The name "Baeckeoffe" translates to "baker's oven," as it was traditionally brought to the local bakery to cook slowly in the residual heat.

Kougelhopf: A beloved Alsatian dessert, kougelhopf is a ring-shaped cake with almonds and raisins, typically served on special occasions.

Alsatian Wines: The region's vineyards produce a wide range of excellent wines, including Riesling, Gewürztraminer, and Pinot Gris. Wine enthusiasts will appreciate the quality and diversity of Alsatian wines, which pair perfectly with local dishes.

The Alsatian culture and gastronomy offer a captivating and flavorful journey through history, traditions, and culinary delights. Exploring this picturesque region and savoring its unique blend of French and German influences is a treat for the senses, leaving visitors with lasting memories of its warmth and charm.

Exploring the Alsace Wine Region

The Alsace wine region, located in northeastern France along the Rhine River, is a picturesque and enchanting destination for wine enthusiasts and travelers alike. With its rolling vineyards, charming villages, and a rich winemaking heritage, Alsace offers a delightful experience for those seeking to explore the world of French wines.

Varietals and Terroir

Alsace is renowned for its exceptional white wines, with Riesling, Gewürztraminer, Pinot Gris, and Muscat being the most celebrated varietals. These wines are known for their aromatic complexity, fruitiness, and superb balance, often reflecting the unique terroir of the region. The Alsace vineyards benefit from a favorable microclimate, with sunny and dry weather conditions that contribute to the grapes' full ripening and flavor development.

Wine Route (Route des Vins d'Alsace)

The Wine Route is the perfect way to explore the region's vineyards and immerse yourself in Alsace's wine culture. Stretching over 170 kilometers (106 miles), the route winds through picturesque villages, offering stunning views of the vine-covered hills. Visitors can stop at numerous wineries along the way to sample a wide array of wines, learn about winemaking techniques, and engage with passionate vintners.

Charming Villages

The Alsace Wine Route takes travelers through a series of charming villages, each with its distinct character and cultural heritage. Villages like Riquewihr, Eguisheim, and Kaysersberg are among the most enchanting, with their half-timbered houses, flower-filled windows, and medieval architecture. Strolling through these villages feels like stepping back in time, creating a romantic and nostalgic ambiance.

Wine Festivals and Events

Throughout the year, Alsace hosts various wine festivals and events that celebrate the region's viticulture. The most famous of these festivals is the Alsace Wine Route Festival (Fête de la Route des Vins d'Alsace), held in August in the village of Ammerschwihr. The festival showcases the best wines of the region, accompanied by music, dancing, and regional cuisine, making it a lively and memorable experience.

Wine and Food Pairings

The Alsace wine region offers a fantastic opportunity to indulge in wine and food pairings that highlight the region's culinary excellence. Local dishes, such as choucroute garnie, flammekueche, and Munster cheese, complement the wines perfectly, enhancing the overall tasting experience.

Historical Wine Cellars

Alsace is home to some of the oldest and most picturesque wine cellars in France. Many wineries offer guided tours of their cellars, allowing visitors to learn about the winemaking process and the aging of wines in oak barrels.

Alsace is a treasure trove for wine lovers, combining scenic beauty, rich history, and a variety of exquisite wines. Exploring the Alsace wine region offers a unique and immersive experience that celebrates the art of winemaking and the charm of French village life, leaving visitors with a lasting appreciation for the region's vinicultural delights.

Basel, Switzerland

Nestled at the crossroads of Switzerland, France, and Germany, Basel is a captivating city that exudes a unique blend of cultural influences. As Switzerland's third-largest city, Basel boasts a rich history, vibrant art scene, and a welcoming atmosphere that draws visitors from around the world. Whether you're exploring its well-preserved medieval old town, admiring world-class art collections, or immersing yourself in the city's diverse cultural offerings, Basel promises an enriching and unforgettable experience.

Art and Culture

Basel is often referred to as the "Cultural Capital of Switzerland" due to its flourishing art scene. The city is home to several renowned art museums, including the Kunstmuseum Basel, which houses an impressive collection of artworks from the Renaissance to contemporary periods. The Fondation Beyeler, located just outside the city, showcases an exquisite collection of modern and contemporary art in a stunning architectural setting. Additionally, the Vitra Design Museum, located nearby in Germany, is a must-visit destination for design enthusiasts.

Historic Old Town

The historic old town of Basel is a charming labyrinth of cobblestone streets, medieval buildings, and lively squares. The Rathaus (Town Hall), with its vibrant red façade and stunning courtyard, is a prominent landmark in the heart of the old town. Nearby, the Münster Cathedral offers breathtaking panoramic views of Basel and the surrounding countryside from its observation deck.

Rhine River and Bridges

The Rhine River gracefully winds through Basel, adding to the city's scenic beauty. Strolling along the riverbanks or taking a boat cruise provides an opportunity to appreciate the city's stunning architecture, including the iconic Middle Bridge (Mittlere Brücke), the oldest bridge in Basel, and the modern and graceful architecture of the Wettstein Bridge.

Basel Fasnacht

Basel's renowned Fasnacht festival is a vibrant and lively celebration of carnival traditions. Held annually in February or March, this three-day event fills the streets with colorful parades, elaborate costumes, and the captivating sound of drums and piccolos. Basel's Fasnacht is considered one of the largest and most spectacular carnivals in Switzerland.

Culinary Delights

Basel offers a diverse culinary scene, with numerous restaurants, cafes, and bars serving a wide array of international cuisines. For an authentic Swiss dining experience, try local specialties like raclette, fondue, and rösti, as well as delectable chocolates and pastries.

Basler Herbstmesse

The Basler Herbstmesse, or Basel Autumn Fair, is one of the oldest and largest fairs in Switzerland. Held in October, this lively event fills the city with funfair rides, game booths, food stalls, and festive entertainment, attracting locals and visitors of all ages.

Basel's unique location and rich cultural offerings make it a captivating destination for travelers seeking an enriching and diverse experience. With its blend of history, art, and vibrant urban life, Basel is a city that leaves a lasting impression on all who venture to explore its delights.

Art and Culture in Basel

Basel, the "Cultural Capital of Switzerland," is a city that pulsates with artistic expression and a vibrant cultural scene. With its impressive array of museums, galleries, theaters, and cultural events, Basel is a haven for art enthusiasts and those seeking a stimulating cultural experience.

Museums

Basel is home to an exceptional collection of world-class museums that cater to various interests and artistic tastes. The Kunstmuseum Basel, founded in 1661, is one of the oldest public art collections in the world and boasts an extensive range of artworks, from the Renaissance to contemporary periods. The museum's collection includes works by renowned artists such as Hans

Holbein the Younger, Rembrandt, Picasso, and Monet.

For modern and contemporary art lovers, the Fondation Beyeler offers a captivating experience. Set amidst a scenic park just outside the city, the museum showcases an impressive collection of artworks by artists like Pablo Picasso, Vincent van Gogh, and Claude Monet, as well as rotating exhibitions of contemporary artists.

The Vitra Design Museum, located a short distance away in Weil am Rhein, Germany, presents a diverse collection of design objects and furniture, celebrating the creativity and innovation of design pioneers.

Cultural Events

Basel hosts a plethora of cultural events and festivals throughout the year, creating a dynamic and engaging atmosphere. One of the most famous events is the Basel Art Basel fair, considered one of the world's premier art fairs, attracting art collectors, curators, and artists from around the globe. Art Basel showcases an extraordinary selection of modern and contemporary art and is a significant event on the international art calendar.

During Fasnacht, Basel's vibrant carnival, the city transforms into a spectacle of color, music, and celebration. This traditional festival, held annually in February or March, fills the streets with elaborately designed costumes, masked performers, and lively processions.

The Basel Tattoo, an international military music festival held in July, features impressive performances by military bands and marching groups from around the world, creating a mesmerizing display of music, choreography, and pageantry.

Theater and Performing Arts

Basel's theater and performing arts scene is equally captivating, with numerous venues presenting a diverse range of theatrical productions, dance performances, concerts, and opera. The Theater Basel is one of the most renowned theaters in Switzerland, offering a diverse program that includes classic plays, contemporary works, and innovative performances.

The Musiksaal at the Stadtcasino Basel hosts performances by the renowned Basel Symphony Orchestra, while the Grand Theatre Basel showcases opera and ballet productions.

Public Art and Street Art

Walking through Basel, visitors will encounter an abundance of public art and street art, adding an artistic dimension to the city's urban landscape.

Basel's public spaces feature sculptures, murals, and installations by both established and emerging artists, making art an integral part of daily life in the city.

Basel's thriving art and culture scene is a testament to the city's rich heritage and its commitment to promoting creativity and artistic expression. Whether exploring world-class museums, attending cultural events, or simply appreciating the art that adorns the streets, Basel offers an enriching and captivating cultural experience for everyone who visits.

Rhine River Cruises in Switzerland

Embarking on a Rhine River cruise in Switzerland offers a mesmerizing journey through some of the most scenic landscapes in Europe. As the majestic Rhine flows through the Swiss countryside, passengers are treated to breathtaking views of snow-capped mountains, charming villages, and lush vineyards. A cruise along the Rhine in Switzerland promises an unforgettable experience, blending natural beauty with cultural discoveries and the comforts of a luxurious river cruise.

Stunning Scenery

The Swiss stretch of the Rhine River meanders through picturesque landscapes that showcase Switzerland's natural beauty. Cruising along the river provides panoramic views of the Swiss Alps, with their towering peaks and cascading waterfalls, creating a postcard-worthy backdrop for the entire journey. The serene and unspoiled surroundings allow passengers to relax and immerse themselves in the tranquil ambiance of the Swiss countryside.

Charming Villages and Towns

The Rhine River cruise takes passengers past enchanting villages and historic towns that exude Old-World charm. Stops along the way might include towns like Stein am Rhein, known for its well-preserved medieval architecture and colorful frescoes adorning its buildings. Schaffhausen, home to the impressive Rhine Falls, offers the opportunity to witness the largest waterfall in Europe up close.

Wine and Vineyards

Switzerland's Rhine region is renowned for its vineyards, and a river cruise provides a unique opportunity to sample some of the country's finest wines. The terraced vineyards that line the riverbanks produce exceptional white wines, particularly Riesling and Pinot Gris. Wine enthusiasts can savor the flavors of the region during onboard wine tastings and shore excursions to local wineries.

Cultural Highlights

A Rhine River cruise in Switzerland offers cultural highlights, with opportunities to explore historical landmarks and immerse oneself in local traditions. Passengers can visit centuries-old castles, such as Schloss Laufen, or explore the charming Old Towns of cities like Basel, with their well-preserved architecture and cultural landmarks.

Comfort and Luxury

Switzerland's Rhine River cruises offer a high level of comfort and luxury on board. Passengers can relax on spacious decks, enjoying the stunning scenery as they glide along the river. The cruise ships are equipped with modern amenities, elegant cabins, and gourmet dining, providing a truly indulgent experience.

Seasonal Beauty

The Rhine River is enchanting year-round, with each season offering its unique allure. Spring brings blossoming flowers and vibrant landscapes, while summer offers warm weather and ample opportunities for outdoor activities. Autumn is a spectacular time for wine enthusiasts, with the vineyards turning hues of red and gold. In winter, the Swiss Alps are covered in a blanket of snow, creating a magical winter wonderland.

A Rhine River cruise in Switzerland is a captivating journey that combines breathtaking natural beauty, cultural discoveries, and luxurious experiences. Whether for leisurely exploration, wine tasting, or simply savoring the tranquility of the Swiss countryside, a cruise along the Rhine promises a truly unforgettable and immersive adventure.

Basel's Unique Architecture

Basel, a city steeped in history and culture, boasts a diverse and captivating architectural landscape. As a hub of artistic expression and architectural innovation, Basel's buildings tell a fascinating story of the city's evolution through the ages. From medieval landmarks to contemporary masterpieces, Basel's unique architecture offers a visual feast for travelers and architecture enthusiasts alike.

Medieval Gems

The old town of Basel is a treasure trove of medieval buildings. The Münster Cathedral, a striking red sandstone masterpiece, dominates the city's skyline with its stunning twin towers. This iconic cathedral, dating back to the 11th century, is a prime example of Romanesque and Gothic architecture and features a beautifully adorned cloister.

The Rathaus (Town Hall) is another architectural gem in the old town. Its vibrant red facade and ornate frescoes make it a visual delight. The Rathaus courtyard, surrounded by arcades and balconies, showcases the city's coat of arms and is a popular spot for gatherings and events.

Modernist Pioneers

Basel has long been a hub for modernist architecture, thanks in part to visionaries like Swiss architects Le Corbusier and Hans Schmidt. Le Corbusier's "Immeuble Clarté" and "Immeuble Molitor" apartment buildings are fine examples of the city's modernist heritage, displaying innovative concrete facades and functionalist design.

Another notable modernist landmark is the Kunstmuseum Basel's extension, designed by renowned architect Renzo Piano. The light-filled, transparent building complements the original museum and provides a seamless link between art and architecture.

Contemporary Wonders

Basel is home to several contemporary architectural wonders that add a dynamic touch to the cityscape. The Vitra Campus, just a short distance from Basel in Weil am Rhein, Germany, is a design lover's dream. This architectural playground features buildings designed by legendary architects such as

Frank Gehry, Zaha Hadid, and Tadao Ando, showcasing innovative and visionary designs.

The Basel Exhibition Center, known as "Messe Basel," boasts contemporary exhibition halls and event spaces with striking modern architecture. Its design versatility allows for a wide range of exhibitions, trade fairs, and cultural events.

Green Architecture

In recent years, Basel has embraced sustainable and eco-friendly architecture, incorporating green spaces and energy-efficient design principles. The Novartis Campus, for example, features modern office buildings with extensive green areas and landscaped gardens, promoting a harmonious balance between nature and architecture.

Basel's unique architecture offers a captivating blend of history, innovation, and creative expression. As you wander through the city's streets, you'll be immersed in a fascinating architectural tapestry that celebrates both the past and the future, making Basel a compelling destination for architectural enthusiasts and travelers seeking to be inspired by the beauty of design.

ONBOARD LIFE

Types of River Cruise Ships

River cruises offer a fantastic way to explore the world's most picturesque waterways and immerse oneself in diverse cultures and landscapes. These cruises come in various styles and sizes, catering to different preferences and travel needs. Here are some common types of river cruise ships:

Classic River Cruise Ships
Classic river cruise ships are the most common type and are often characterized by their elegant and timeless design. These ships typically feature a mix of staterooms and suites with varying amenities, offering a comfortable and relaxing onboard experience. Passengers can enjoy panoramic views of the river and its surroundings from the ship's sun decks and lounges. Classic river cruises often focus on cultural excursions and immersive experiences at various ports of call.

Luxury River Cruise Ships
Luxury river cruise ships offer a more indulgent and opulent experience. These ships are known for their spacious and lavishly appointed suites, personalized service, and top-notch amenities. Onboard fine dining, butler service, and exclusive excursions are

often included in the luxury river cruise experience. Passengers seeking a pampered and upscale journey will find these ships to be the epitome of luxury travel on the water.

Boutique River Cruise Ships

Boutique river cruise ships are small and intimate vessels that cater to a limited number of passengers, creating an intimate and personalized atmosphere. These ships often have unique designs and are crafted to blend seamlessly with the local surroundings. Boutique river cruises provide a more immersive and boutique-style experience, often emphasizing cultural immersion and regional cuisine.

Expedition River Cruise Ships

For travelers seeking adventure and exploration, expedition river cruise ships are an ideal choice. These ships are designed to navigate more remote and lesser-explored waterways, allowing passengers to discover hidden gems and off-the-beaten-path destinations. Expedition cruises often include activities such as wildlife spotting, hiking, and interacting with local communities.

Theme and Special Interest River Cruise Ships

Theme and special interest river cruises cater to travelers with specific interests, such as art, wine, history, or music. These cruises offer specialized itineraries, onboard lectures, workshops, and excursions tailored to the chosen theme. Whether it's an art-focused cruise along the Danube or a wine-themed cruise in Bordeaux, these sailings provide a deeper dive into the chosen subject.

Family-Friendly River Cruise Ships

Family-friendly river cruise ships cater to multi-generational travel and offer amenities and activities suitable for all ages. These cruises may include family cabins, onboard entertainment for kids, and age-appropriate shore excursions. Family-friendly river cruises provide a memorable and hassle-free experience for families seeking to explore together.

No matter the type of river cruise ship you choose, a river cruise promises an enriching and unforgettable journey, allowing travelers to discover the world's most beautiful waterways and the diverse cultures that line their banks.

Accommodation Options

River cruises offer a variety of accommodation options to suit different preferences and budgets. Whether you're seeking a cozy and intimate atmosphere or luxurious indulgence, river cruise ships provide a range of staterooms and suites to make your journey comfortable and enjoyable. Here are some common accommodation options on river cruises:

Standard Staterooms

Standard staterooms are the most common and affordable accommodation option on river cruises. These cozy cabins typically offer essential amenities, such as a comfortable bed, a private bathroom, and storage space for your belongings. While they may be more compact compared to larger suites, standard staterooms provide a comfortable and practical space for resting and relaxing after a day of exploring.

Balcony Staterooms

Balcony staterooms offer an added level of luxury and convenience. In addition to standard amenities, these staterooms feature a private balcony or a French balcony, allowing passengers to enjoy stunning river views from the comfort of their own space. Balcony staterooms provide an intimate connection to the passing scenery and offer a serene spot to unwind and take in the sights.

Suites

Suites on river cruises are the epitome of luxury and indulgence. These spacious and well-appointed accommodations often come with additional amenities, such as larger living areas, separate sleeping and sitting areas, and luxurious bathrooms. Suites may also include personalized butler service and access to exclusive facilities, such as private lounges and dining venues.

Family Cabins

Family cabins are designed to accommodate families and groups traveling together. These cabins often feature extra space, with multiple beds and additional storage to accommodate the needs of families. Family-friendly river cruises may also offer connecting cabins to ensure that everyone can stay together comfortably.

Solo Traveler Cabins

For solo travelers, some river cruise ships offer dedicated solo traveler cabins. These cabins are designed for single occupancy, providing the privacy and comfort solo travelers seek without the burden of a single supplement fee. Solo traveler cabins are a great option for those who prefer to explore the world on their own terms.

Wheelchair-Accessible Cabins

Many modern river cruise ships provide wheelchair-accessible cabins to accommodate passengers with mobility challenges. These cabins are designed with wider doorways, accessible bathrooms, and other features to ensure a comfortable and convenient stay for all passengers.

No matter the type of accommodation you choose, river cruises offer a comfortable and convenient way to explore scenic waterways and immerse yourself in the beauty and culture of your chosen destination.

Dining and Cuisine

One of the highlights of a river cruise is the delectable dining experience it offers to passengers. From indulging in regional specialties to savoring international cuisines, river cruises take passengers on a culinary journey that complements the cultural exploration of the destinations visited. Here's what you can expect when it comes to dining and cuisine on river cruises:

Gourmet Meals

River cruise ships pride themselves on providing gourmet meals that rival the finest restaurants. Expert chefs curate a diverse and delightful menu, incorporating fresh and locally sourced ingredients. From breakfast to dinner, passengers can expect a sumptuous array of dishes that cater to various tastes and dietary preferences.

Regional Specialties

One of the highlights of river cruise dining is the opportunity to sample authentic regional specialties at each destination. As the ship sails through different regions, the onboard menus reflect the local flavors and culinary traditions. Whether it's trying schnitzel in Austria, coq au vin in France, or risotto in Italy, passengers can indulge in the true essence of each region's cuisine.

Open Seating

Most river cruises offer open seating arrangements, allowing passengers to dine at their preferred time and sit wherever they wish. This flexible approach fosters a relaxed and congenial atmosphere, where guests can mingle and share their travel experiences over a delicious meal.

Complimentary Drinks

Many river cruise lines include complimentary drinks during mealtimes, such as regional wines, beer, and soft drinks. This adds to the all-inclusive nature of river cruises and allows passengers to pair their meals with the perfect beverage.

Special Dining Events

River cruises often feature special dining events to enhance the onboard experience. These events may include chef-led cooking demonstrations, themed dinners, and tastings of local wines or cheeses. Passengers can partake in interactive culinary experiences that enrich their understanding and appreciation of the local cuisine.

Dining Venues

River cruise ships typically offer multiple dining venues, each with its own ambiance and menu. The main dining room serves as the primary venue for breakfast, lunch, and dinner, offering a wide selection of dishes in a more formal setting. Additionally, some ships feature specialty restaurants, where passengers can enjoy intimate dining experiences with carefully curated menus.

Vegetarian and Dietary Options

River cruises are attentive to dietary preferences and requirements. Whether you're a vegetarian, have food allergies, or follow specific dietary restrictions, cruise lines are generally happy to accommodate your needs. Prior notification of dietary requirements ensures that the ship's culinary team can cater to your preferences.

Room Service

For those seeking a more intimate dining experience, many river cruise ships offer room service. Passengers can enjoy meals or snacks in the comfort of their own staterooms, taking advantage of the ship's exceptional culinary offerings at any time of the day.

The dining experience on a river cruise is not merely about sustenance but a journey of flavors and cultural discovery. It's an opportunity to savor the essence of the destinations visited, bringing a world of culinary delights to your plate as you glide along the serene waterways.

Entertainment and Activities

River cruises offer a delightful array of entertainment and activities to keep passengers engaged and entertained throughout their journey. From cultural performances to enriching lectures, and from leisurely pursuits to immersive excursions, river cruises cater to diverse interests and preferences. Here are some of the entertainment and activities you can expect on a river cruise:

Cultural Performances

River cruises often feature onboard cultural performances that showcase the local traditions and music of the regions visited. These performances may include live music, dance shows, and folkloric displays, offering passengers a taste of the authentic cultural heritage of each destination.

Educational Lectures and Workshops

River cruises provide opportunities for passengers to engage in educational and enriching activities. Lectures by guest speakers, historians, and experts on board delve into the history, art, and culture of the regions visited. Workshops may include cooking demonstrations, language lessons, or handicraft classes, allowing passengers to immerse themselves in the local way of life.

Live Music and Entertainment

Evenings on a river cruise often feature live music and entertainment to create a vibrant and enjoyable atmosphere. From piano recitals and jazz performances to themed parties and dancing, there's always something to keep passengers entertained after a day of exploration.

Scenic Cruising and Sun Decks

River cruises offer the perfect opportunity to soak in the breathtaking scenery as the ship glides along the waterways. Passengers can relax on the ship's sun decks, enjoying panoramic views of riverside landscapes, castles, and charming villages. Scenic cruising allows for a leisurely and immersive experience, creating moments of serenity and tranquility.

Excursions and Shore Activities

One of the highlights of a river cruise is the chance to explore the destinations visited through a variety of shore excursions and activities. Guided city tours, visits to historical landmarks, wine tastings, and culinary experiences are just some of the options available. These excursions provide an enriching and immersive experience, allowing passengers to connect with the local culture and traditions.

Fitness and Wellness

For those seeking to stay active during their cruise, river ships often provide fitness facilities, including gyms and wellness centers. Passengers can participate in yoga classes, fitness sessions, or take a dip in the ship's swimming pool.

Culinary Experiences

River cruises may offer culinary experiences onboard, such as cooking classes or tastings of regional dishes and wines. Passengers can learn the art of preparing local delicacies and enjoy the flavors of the regions they are sailing through.

Casual Games and Entertainment

River cruise ships provide casual games and entertainment options for leisurely enjoyment. Passengers can participate in board games, trivia contests, or relax with a good book from the onboard library.

The variety of entertainment and activities on a river cruise ensures that passengers have a fulfilling and enjoyable experience as they explore the picturesque waterways and the cultural gems that line their banks. Whether seeking relaxation or adventure, a river cruise promises a perfect blend of entertainment and enrichment for all passengers to cherish and savor.

Wellness and Spa Facilities

River cruises have evolved to cater to the holistic well-being of passengers, offering a range of wellness and spa facilities that promote relaxation, rejuvenation, and a sense of tranquility throughout the journey. These onboard amenities provide the perfect complement to the cultural exploration and immersive experiences onshore. Here are some common wellness and spa facilities offered on river cruises:

Spa Centers

River cruise ships often feature spa centers equipped with various amenities to pamper passengers. Spa facilities may include steam rooms, saunas, whirlpools, and relaxation lounges. After a day of exploration, passengers can unwind in these soothing environments, easing tired muscles and revitalizing the senses.

Massage and Beauty Treatments

Professional massage therapists offer a variety of massage treatments designed to ease tension and promote relaxation. From Swedish massages to hot stone therapies, passengers can indulge in rejuvenating spa treatments that enhance their overall well-being. Beauty treatments such as facials, manicures, and pedicures are also available for those seeking to pamper themselves.

Fitness Centers and Yoga Studios

Many river cruise ships are equipped with fitness centers featuring state-of-the-art equipment for passengers who wish to maintain their workout routines while cruising. Yoga studios may also be available, offering classes with scenic views of the passing landscapes. Participating in fitness activities can help guests stay active and energized during their journey.

Wellness Classes and Workshops

River cruises often offer wellness classes and workshops led by experts in various disciplines. These may include yoga sessions, meditation classes, or even wellness talks on topics like nutrition and healthy living. Passengers have the opportunity to engage in activities that promote mindfulness and overall health.

Sun Decks and Outdoor Spaces

River cruise ships provide ample outdoor spaces, such as sun decks, where passengers can bask in the fresh air and enjoy the picturesque views. Loungers and seating areas are ideal for relaxation and moments of quiet contemplation.

Healthy Dining Options

In addition to spa facilities, river cruise ships offer healthy dining options that cater to passengers' wellness needs. Menus may include nutritious and light dishes, as well as vegetarian and vegan choices, ensuring that passengers can maintain a balanced diet while on their journey.

Wellness Concierge Services

Some river cruise lines provide dedicated wellness concierge services to assist passengers in customizing their wellness experiences. The wellness concierge can help passengers plan their spa treatments, fitness routines, and wellness activities, ensuring a seamless and fulfilling experience.

River cruises offer an ideal setting for passengers to prioritize self-care and well-being while exploring the world's most scenic waterways. Whether it's indulging in spa treatments, practicing yoga on the sun deck, or enjoying healthy dining options, the wellness and spa facilities on river cruises provide a serene sanctuary for passengers seeking relaxation and rejuvenation.

What to Pack for a Rhine River Cruise

Packing for a Rhine River cruise requires careful consideration to ensure you have everything you need for a comfortable and enjoyable journey. From exploring charming towns to scenic cruising along the river, here's a comprehensive list of items to pack for your Rhine River cruise:

Clothing
- Casual daytime attire (comfortable clothing for shore excursions and walking tours)
- Dressier outfits for evening dinners and special events (optional)
- Layers (lightweight sweaters, scarves, and jackets) for changing weather conditions
- Raincoat or waterproof jacket

- Comfortable walking shoes or sneakers
- Dress shoes (for evening dinners or events)
- Swimsuit (some ships have onboard pools or hot tubs)
- Pajamas and loungewear

Personal Essentials
- Passport and other travel documents
- Travel insurance information
- Prescription medications and any necessary medical supplies
- Personal toiletries (shampoo, conditioner, soap, etc.)
- Sunscreen and lip balm with SPF
- Insect repellent (depending on the season)
- Sunglasses and a wide-brimmed hat for sun protection
- Prescription eyeglasses or contact lenses (plus a spare pair)
- Travel adapter and chargers for electronic devices

Day Bag
- A small backpack or tote bag for carrying essentials during shore excursions
- Refillable water bottle
- Camera or smartphone for capturing memories

- Binoculars for scenic views and wildlife spotting
- Guidebook or map of the destinations you'll visit
- Travel journal and pen

Travel Accessories
- Luggage tags with your contact information
- Travel locks for added security
- Travel blanket and pillow for additional comfort on lengthy journeys
- Earplugs and an eye mask for a restful sleep
- Lightweight umbrella (in case of rain)
- Foldable shopping bag for souvenirs and local purchases.

Formal Nights (if applicable)
- Some river cruise lines may have formal or dressy evenings. Check with your cruise line to see if formal attire is required and pack accordingly (e.g., cocktail dresses, suits, ties).

Personal Medications and First Aid
- Bring any prescribed medications you regularly take, along with a copy of the prescription.

- Pack a small first aid kit with basic supplies like band-aids, pain relievers, antacids, and motion sickness medication.

Remember to pack light and efficiently, as most river cruise cabins have limited storage space. Many river cruises have casual dress codes, so focus on comfortable and versatile clothing suitable for various weather conditions. Additionally, check with your specific cruise line for any dress code requirements or recommendations.

With these essentials packed, you'll be well-prepared to embark on a memorable Rhine River cruise, filled with exploration, relaxation, and the enchanting sights of the beautiful river and its surrounding landscapes.

THE RHINE RIVER CRUISE EXPERIENCE

Daily Itinerary and Activities

Day 1: Embarkation in Basel, Switzerland

Arrive in Basel and board your river cruise ship.

After settling into your stateroom, join a welcome cocktail reception to meet fellow passengers and the crew.

Enjoy a delectable dinner onboard as the ship sets sail for your Rhine River adventure.

Day 2: Strasbourg, France

Wake up in Strasbourg, a captivating city known for its half-timbered houses and the iconic Strasbourg Cathedral.

Embark on a guided walking tour to explore the charming streets of Strasbourg's historic Old Town, La Petite France, and the picturesque canals.

Enjoy some free time to discover the local shops, cafés, and sample Alsatian delights.

Return to the ship for dinner and evening entertainment, which might include a cultural performance or themed event.

Day 3: Heidelberg, Germany

Arrive in Heidelberg, famous for its majestic castle and historic university.

Take a guided tour of Heidelberg Castle, with its stunning views of the city and the Neckar River.

Explore the enchanting streets of the Old Town, filled with charming shops and cafés.

In the afternoon, enjoy leisure time or optional excursions, such as a scenic bike ride or a visit to a local vineyard for wine tasting.

Return to the ship for dinner and relaxation as you continue your journey.

Day 4: Rhine Gorge and Rüdesheim, Germany

Cruise through the picturesque Rhine Gorge, a UNESCO World Heritage Site known for its stunning landscapes, castles, and vineyards.

Arrive in Rüdesheim and visit Siegfried's Mechanical Music Cabinet, a fascinating museum showcasing mechanical musical instruments.

Stroll along the lively Drosselgasse street, known for its wine taverns and live music.

Take a cable car ride to the Niederwald Monument for breathtaking views of the Rhine River valley.

Enjoy dinner onboard and perhaps partake in a wine tasting event showcasing local German wines.

Day 5: Cologne, Germany

Arrive in Cologne, home to the iconic Cologne Cathedral (Kölner Dom).

Take a guided tour of the magnificent cathedral, a masterpiece of Gothic architecture.

Explore the historic Old Town, visit local markets, and sample traditional Kölsch beer.

In the evening, return to the ship for dinner and evening entertainment, which may include a themed party or live music.

Day 6: Amsterdam, Netherlands

Arrive in Amsterdam, the vibrant capital of the Netherlands.

Take a guided canal cruise to admire Amsterdam's picturesque canals, bridges, and historic buildings.

Visit famous landmarks such as the Anne Frank House and the Rijksmuseum.

Enjoy free time to explore Amsterdam's lively neighborhoods, visit museums, or take a bike ride through the city.

Return to the ship for a farewell dinner, reminiscing about the memorable experiences of your Rhine River cruise.

Day 7: Disembarkation in Amsterdam

After breakfast, disembark in Amsterdam and bid farewell to your newfound friends and the crew.

Transfer to the airport or extend your stay to explore more of this captivating city at your leisure.

Please note that this itinerary is a sample and may vary based on the cruise line, departure date, and specific ship. River cruises provide a balance of guided tours and free time, allowing you to customize your daily activities according to your interests and preferences.

Shore Excursions and Guided Tours

A Rhine River cruise offers an array of captivating shore excursions and guided tours, allowing passengers to immerse themselves in the rich history, culture, and natural beauty of the destinations along the river. These expertly curated experiences enhance the overall journey, providing passengers with in-depth insights and memorable moments. Here are some of the shore excursions and guided tours you can expect on a Rhine River cruise:

City Walking Tours

Explore the charming towns and cities that line the Rhine River with guided walking tours. Knowledgeable local guides lead you through historic old towns, past medieval landmarks, and along picturesque streets. Discover the fascinating stories behind iconic landmarks and gain a deeper understanding of the region's heritage.

Castles and Palaces

Journey back in time with visits to the majestic castles and palaces that dot the Rhine Valley. Guided tours take you to stunning hilltop fortresses with breathtaking views of the river and the surrounding landscapes. Learn about the captivating history of these medieval structures and the tales of knights and nobles that once inhabited them.

Vineyard Visits and Wine Tastings

The Rhine Valley is renowned for its vineyards and world-class wines. Embark on excursions to local wineries and vineyards, where you'll learn about the winemaking process and indulge in wine tastings. Savor the unique flavors of regional wines, such as Riesling and Pinot Noir.

Culinary Experiences

Immerse yourself in the local gastronomy with culinary-themed excursions. Join cooking classes led by expert chefs to learn how to prepare traditional dishes. Experience food markets to sample regional delicacies and local specialties, such as cheese, sausages, and pastries.

UNESCO World Heritage Sites

The Rhine River region is home to several UNESCO World Heritage Sites. Guided tours take you to these extraordinary sites, such as the Cologne Cathedral, the Strasbourg Grand Île, and the Upper Middle Rhine Valley. Explore the cultural and historical significance of these revered landmarks.

Scenic Cruising and Nature Walks

Enjoy leisurely scenic cruises along the Rhine River, taking in the breathtaking landscapes, vineyard-covered hills, and charming villages along the banks. Some river cruises may offer nature walks or hikes through the picturesque countryside, allowing you to appreciate the natural beauty up close.

Art and Museum Visits

Discover the artistic heritage of the region with visits to art museums and galleries. Guided tours provide insights into the works of famous artists, such as those showcased at the Kunstmuseum Basel, and contemporary exhibits that celebrate creativity.

Active Adventures

For the more adventurous, river cruises may offer active excursions like bike tours, hiking expeditions, or kayaking excursions. These adventures allow you to experience the region's landscapes from a different perspective and get closer to nature.

Shore excursions and guided tours on a Rhine River cruise cater to various interests and preferences, ensuring that passengers have a well-rounded and immersive experience.

Scenic Highlights and Photo Opportunities

A Rhine River cruise is a photographer's dream, offering a plethora of scenic highlights and photo opportunities at every turn. From medieval castles perched atop vineyard-covered hills to charming towns with cobblestone streets, the picturesque landscapes along the Rhine provide endless inspiration for capturing stunning images. Here are some of the scenic highlights and photo opportunities you can look forward to on your Rhine River cruise:

Rhine Gorge

Cruising through the scenic Rhine Gorge is a highlight of any river cruise. This UNESCO World Heritage Site is characterized by dramatic landscapes, steep vineyards, and the legendary Lorelei Rock. Keep your camera ready to capture the charming castles that dot the hillsides, creating a fairytale-like atmosphere.

Castles and Fortresses

The Rhine Valley is renowned for its impressive castles and fortresses, many of which are well-preserved and perched atop picturesque hills. From the iconic Marksburg Castle to the majestic Rheinfels Castle, these historic landmarks provide excellent photo opportunities, especially during scenic cruising.

Strasbourg's Canals

Strasbourg's La Petite France district, with its charming half-timbered houses and quaint canals, is a photographer's delight. Stroll along the narrow cobblestone streets and capture reflections of the colorful buildings in the tranquil waters of the canals.

Cologne Cathedral

The awe-inspiring Cologne Cathedral (Kölner Dom) is a masterpiece of Gothic architecture and a must-see landmark in Cologne. Photograph the intricate details of its façade and the soaring spires that dominate the skyline.

Windmills of Kinderdijk

When visiting Kinderdijk in the Netherlands, be sure to photograph the iconic windmills that have become synonymous with Dutch landscapes. These well-preserved windmills, dating back to the 18th century, create a picturesque scene against the horizon.

Vineyard-Covered Hills

As you sail along the river, you'll be treated to sweeping views of terraced vineyards covering the hillsides. During the autumn season, the vineyards turn hues of gold and red, making for a stunning photo backdrop.

Amsterdam's Canals and Bridges

Explore Amsterdam's canal belt, a UNESCO World Heritage Site, and capture images of the city's charming canals lined with historic buildings and picturesque bridges. Photograph the unique architecture and the reflections of the city in the tranquil waters.

Cochem's Fairytale Scenery

Cochem, a charming town nestled in the Moselle Valley, offers fairytale-like scenery. Photograph the colorful buildings huddled around the Cochem Castle, set against a backdrop of vineyards and rolling hills.

Romantic Rhine River Sunsets

The Rhine River provides the perfect setting for capturing breathtaking sunsets. Watch as the sun sets over the river, casting a golden glow over the landscapes and creating a magical atmosphere.

Remember to keep your camera or smartphone handy throughout the cruise, as the scenic highlights and photo opportunities along the Rhine River are bound to present themselves at any moment. Capture the beauty of the landscapes, the architectural wonders, and the cultural gems that grace the riverbanks, creating lasting memories of your remarkable Rhine River cruise.

Interacting with Locals along the Rhine

One of the most rewarding aspects of a Rhine River cruise is the opportunity to interact with the friendly locals who call the river's picturesque banks home. From bustling cities to charming villages, the Rhine Valley is dotted with communities eager to share their culture, traditions, and warm hospitality with visitors. Here are some ways you can engage with locals and create meaningful connections during your Rhine River cruise:

Exploring Local Markets

Venture into bustling local markets, where you'll find fresh produce, handcrafted goods, and regional delicacies. Engage in friendly conversations with vendors, learn about their products, and sample local treats. Whether it's tasting artisan cheeses, trying freshly baked bread, or purchasing unique souvenirs, these interactions offer a glimpse into everyday life in the region.

Participating in Local Festivals

If your cruise coincides with local festivals or events, don't miss the chance to join the celebrations. Festivals offer a wonderful opportunity to immerse yourself in the local culture, witness traditional performances, and join in the festivities. Whether it's a wine festival, a music concert, or a traditional fair, you'll experience the vibrant spirit of the community firsthand.

Attending Workshops and Demonstrations

Many destinations along the Rhine offer workshops and demonstrations that provide insight into local craftsmanship and traditions. Join artisans to learn pottery, wood carving, or other traditional crafts. Interacting with skilled locals allows you to appreciate the talent and dedication behind these age-old practices.

Visiting Local Cafés and Pubs

To truly experience the essence of a region, spend some time in local cafés and pubs. Strike up conversations with locals over a cup of coffee or a pint of local beer. You'll gain insights into their daily lives, local customs, and perhaps even receive recommendations on hidden gems to explore.

Learning the Language

Connecting with locals might be facilitated by learning a few fundamental phrases in their language. Greetings, thank-yous, and simple expressions of appreciation show respect and demonstrate your interest in their culture. Locals often appreciate the effort, and it can lead to more engaging interactions.

Taking Part in Cultural Experiences

Participate in cultural experiences offered during excursions or as part of the cruise program. Whether it's a traditional dance performance, a wine tasting session, or a cooking class, these activities provide unique opportunities to bond with locals and gain a deeper understanding of their way of life.

Expressing Curiosity and Respect

Approach interactions with an open mind and a genuine curiosity about the local culture. Respect local customs and traditions, and be sensitive to cultural differences. Demonstrating a genuine interest in learning about the local way of life will often lead to warm and welcoming interactions.

Engaging with locals along the Rhine River enriches your travel experience, creating lasting memories and meaningful connections.

RHINE RIVER CRUISING TIPS

Money-Saving Strategies

While a Rhine River cruise offers a luxurious and enriching travel experience, it's natural to seek ways to make the most of your budget without compromising on the quality of your journey. Here are some money-saving strategies to help you get the best value from your Rhine River cruise:

Book Early

Booking your Rhine River cruise well in advance can often result in significant savings. Cruise lines often offer early booking discounts, allowing you to secure the best prices and cabin options.

Look for Special Deals and Offers

Keep an eye out for special deals and promotions offered by cruise lines. Look for discounts on specific sailings, reduced or waived single supplement fees for solo travelers, or offers that include complimentary excursions or beverage packages.

Consider Shoulder Seasons

Traveling during the shoulder seasons (spring and fall) can often lead to lower cruise prices compared to peak summer months. You can still enjoy pleasant weather and fewer crowds while saving on your cruise fare.

All-Inclusive Packages

Consider choosing an all-inclusive river cruise package that includes meals, drinks, excursions, and onboard amenities. While the upfront cost might be higher, all-inclusive packages can save you money in the long run by covering most of your expenses.

Group Travel

Some cruise lines offer discounts for group bookings. Consider traveling with family or friends to take advantage of group rates, which can help reduce the per-person cost.

Opt for Interior Cabins

If you're looking to save on accommodation, consider booking an interior cabin or a stateroom with a lower category. While you might miss out on scenic views from your room, you'll still have access to all the ship's amenities and public areas with stunning views.

DIY Excursions

While guided excursions provided by the cruise line offer convenience, consider exploring some destinations on your own. Research and plan self-guided tours to explore the towns and cities at your own pace, which can save you money on excursion fees.

Set a Budget for Onboard Spending

Determine a budget for onboard spending, such as drinks, spa treatments, and souvenirs. By setting limits, you can avoid overspending and keep track of your expenses throughout the cruise.

Avoid Unnecessary Expenses

Be mindful of optional add-ons and purchases during the cruise. While it's tempting to indulge in every experience, consider which extras truly add value to your journey and prioritize accordingly.

Take Advantage of Included Amenities

Make the most of the included amenities on your river cruise ship, such as onboard entertainment, fitness facilities, and complimentary Wi-Fi. These amenities provide additional value without extra cost.

By combining these money-saving strategies, you can enjoy a memorable and budget-conscious Rhine River cruise. Remember that while saving money is essential, the experiences and memories you create during your journey are what truly make the trip priceless.

Language and Communication

A Rhine River cruise provides a unique opportunity to explore multiple countries and experience different cultures along the river's scenic route. As you journey through diverse regions, you'll encounter various languages and communication styles. Here are some essential aspects to consider regarding language and communication during your Rhine River cruise:

Multilingual Crew

Most river cruise ships employ a multilingual crew capable of speaking English and other languages. English is typically the primary language used for announcements, safety instructions, and onboard activities. The crew's language proficiency ensures that passengers from different countries can communicate effectively with the ship's staff.

Guided Tours

Shore excursions and guided tours organized by the cruise line often include knowledgeable local guides who speak fluent English. They provide insightful commentary and explanations about the history, culture, and landmarks of the destinations visited.

Language Barriers

While English is widely spoken in the tourism industry, particularly in Europe, you may encounter language barriers when interacting with locals during independent explorations. Learning a few basic phrases in the local language, such as greetings and thank-yous, can go a long way in showing respect and building rapport with locals.

Language of the Host Country

Each destination along the Rhine River may have its own official language. For example, in Germany, German is spoken, while in France, French is the primary language. It's helpful to familiarize yourself with basic phrases and common words of the host country to navigate everyday interactions.

Onboard Translation Services

Some river cruise lines provide translation services for guests who speak languages other than English. This may include translating printed materials, such as daily activity schedules and menus, into multiple languages.

Communication Apps

Consider using translation apps on your smartphone to bridge language gaps during your travels. These apps can be helpful for translating written text, signs, and menus in real-time.

Cultural Awareness

When interacting with locals, cultural awareness is essential. Different cultures may have varying communication styles and customs. Be respectful of local traditions and customs, and approach interactions with an open mind and willingness to learn about different ways of life.

Non-Verbal Communication

In situations where language barriers may exist, non-verbal communication can play a significant role. A smile, a nod, or a gesture of appreciation can convey goodwill and foster positive interactions.

Remember that a river cruise along the Rhine River is a fantastic opportunity to connect with people from different backgrounds and embrace cultural diversity.

Safety and Security

Safety and security are paramount concerns for both travelers and cruise operators during a Rhine River cruise. Cruise lines take extensive measures to ensure the well-being and comfort of passengers throughout their journey. Here are some important aspects of safety and security to consider during your Rhine River cruise:

Experienced Crew and Staff

River cruise ships are staffed with experienced and well-trained crew members who are knowledgeable about safety protocols and procedures. They undergo rigorous training to handle emergency situations and ensure passenger safety.

Life-Saving Equipment

All river cruise ships are equipped with life-saving equipment, including life jackets, lifeboats, and life rafts. Passengers receive safety briefings at the beginning of the cruise, detailing the location and proper use of safety equipment.

Onboard Safety Drills

Before the ship departs, mandatory safety drills are conducted to familiarize passengers with emergency procedures, muster stations, and evacuation routes.

These drills are essential to ensure everyone is prepared in case of an emergency.

Safety Regulations and Compliance

River cruise ships adhere to strict safety regulations and guidelines set forth by international maritime organizations. These regulations cover everything from ship design and construction to operational protocols and emergency response procedures.

Health and Hygiene Measures

In light of health concerns, river cruise lines have implemented enhanced hygiene protocols to safeguard the health of passengers and crew. These measures may include increased cleaning and sanitization of public areas, hand sanitizing stations throughout the ship, and health screenings as needed.

Port Security

At each port of call, the ship follows port security protocols to ensure the safety of passengers and crew during embarkation and disembarkation. Cruise lines work closely with port authorities to maintain a secure environment.

Local Safety Considerations

While the Rhine River region is generally safe for travelers, it's essential to be aware of your surroundings and take standard precautions, such as safeguarding valuables and avoiding poorly lit or isolated areas during independent explorations in ports.

Emergency Medical Services

River cruise ships are equipped with medical facilities and have trained medical personnel onboard to handle any health emergencies. Additionally, they can coordinate with local medical facilities in case further medical attention is required.

Travel Insurance

Before embarking on a Rhine River cruise, consider purchasing comprehensive travel insurance that covers medical emergencies, trip cancellations, and other unforeseen events. Additional security and comfort are offered by travel insurance.

Staying Informed

Stay informed about safety procedures, changes in the itinerary, and any updates from the cruise line. Pay attention to announcements and notices provided by the ship's crew to ensure a safe and enjoyable journey.

By following these safety guidelines and staying vigilant during your Rhine River cruise, you can focus on the enriching experiences and breathtaking landscapes, knowing that your safety and security are a top priority for the cruise line.

Etiquette and Cultural Considerations

A Rhine River cruise takes you through diverse cultures and countries, each with its own unique customs and etiquette. Being respectful and considerate of local traditions enhances your travel experience and fosters positive interactions with both fellow travelers and the welcoming locals you encounter. Here are some important etiquette and cultural considerations to keep in mind during your Rhine River cruise:

Greetings

In many European countries, a handshake is a common way to greet others. Be sure to offer a friendly handshake when meeting new people, including fellow passengers, crew members, and locals. In more formal settings, a simple nod or smile is often appropriate.

Dress Code

Respect the dress codes on and off the ship. While river cruises are generally casual affairs, some evening dinners or events may call for dressier attire. Additionally, when visiting religious sites or conservative areas, dressing modestly is recommended.

Language Considerations

Learning a few basic phrases in the local language, such as greetings and thank-yous, is appreciated by locals and can help you connect on a deeper level.

While English is widely spoken, making an effort to communicate in the local language shows respect for the local culture.

Tipping

Tipping practices vary across countries and cruise lines. On some river cruises, gratuities may be included in the cruise fare, while on others, they may be left to the discretion of passengers. Familiarize yourself with the tipping policy of your specific cruise line to avoid any confusion.

Dining Etiquette

When dining on the ship or in local restaurants, be mindful of dining etiquette. Wait for everyone at your table to be served before starting to eat, and use utensils appropriately based on local customs. In some cultures, leaving a small amount of food on your plate is a sign of appreciation.

Cultural Sensitivity

Respect local customs, traditions, and religious practices. Be aware of and adhere to any rules or restrictions in places of worship, and avoid taking photographs in sensitive areas unless permitted. Additionally, respect local customs regarding photography of people.

Personal Space

Respect personal space when interacting with both fellow passengers and locals. Different cultures may have varying norms for personal boundaries, so be mindful of personal space preferences.

Punctuality

Be punctual for scheduled activities, excursions, and tours. Arriving on time shows respect for your fellow passengers and the guides who are leading the tours.

Politeness and Courtesies

Simple acts of politeness, such as saying "please" and "thank you" and using courteous language, go a long way in fostering positive interactions with both passengers and locals.

Photography

When taking photos of people, ask for permission first, especially when photographing locals or during guided tours. Be respectful of people's privacy and refrain from taking photos in places where photography is prohibited.

By being culturally aware and practicing good etiquette during your Rhine River cruise, you will not only ensure a smoother and more enjoyable travel experience but also show respect for the rich cultural diversity that makes the journey along the Rhine so enriching.

Photography Tips for Capturing the Scenery

A Rhine River cruise offers breathtaking scenery at every turn, from picturesque villages and historic castles to rolling vineyards and charming cities. Capturing the beauty of these landscapes through photography allows you to preserve your memories and share the enchanting experience with others. Here are some photography tips to help you make the most of your scenic Rhine River cruise:

Use the Right Gear

Consider bringing a versatile camera with manual settings, such as a digital single-lens reflex (DSLR) camera or a mirrorless camera. These cameras give you greater control over exposure, focus, and composition, allowing you to capture the stunning landscapes in their best light.

Shoot During Golden Hour

The "golden hour," which occurs shortly after sunrise and just before sunset, provides soft, warm light that enhances the beauty of the scenery. Take advantage of this magical time for the most stunning and atmospheric photos.

Frame Your Shots

Use natural elements, such as overhanging tree branches, archways, or doorways, to frame your compositions. Framing adds depth and draws the viewer's eye into the scene, creating more captivating photographs.

Focus on Details

While capturing the grand vistas is essential, don't forget to focus on the small details that make the scenery unique. Zoom in on intricate architectural features, colorful flowers, or interesting textures to add variety to your photo collection.

Incorporate Reflections

The Rhine River and its tributaries provide opportunities for stunning reflections. Capture mirror-like reflections of castles and buildings on the water's surface, particularly during calm weather.

Use Leading Lines

Look for natural leading lines, such as riverside paths, rows of vines, or bridges, that guide the viewer's gaze into the photo and towards the main subject.

Experiment with Angles

Vary your shooting angles to find the most appealing perspectives. Try shooting from low angles to add a sense of depth or from higher vantage points to showcase the vastness of the landscapes.

Include People

Adding people to your photographs can provide a sense of scale and human interest. Include fellow passengers, locals, or even yourself to create a connection between the viewer and the scene.

Be Patient and Observant

Scenic opportunities can arise unexpectedly, so stay observant and be patient. Keep your camera ready, as you may encounter beautiful scenes, wildlife, or unique moments during your journey.

Edit Thoughtfully

Post-processing can enhance the impact of your photos. Make exposure, contrast, and color balance adjustments using editing software. However, aim to retain the natural beauty of the scenery and avoid over-editing, which can result in unrealistic or artificial-looking images.

Most importantly, enjoy the process of capturing the scenery on your Rhine River cruise. Take time to appreciate the stunning landscapes and immerse yourself in the enchanting surroundings. With these photography tips, you'll be able to create a collection of images that reflect the beauty and magic of your journey along the Rhine River.

BEYOND THE CRUISE: EXTENDING YOUR TRIP

Additional Days in Departure Cities

If you have the opportunity, consider extending your stay in the departure cities of your Rhine River cruise. These cities are not only gateways to the scenic river journey but also hold their own charm and cultural treasures. Taking extra days in these cities allows you to explore their unique attractions, immerse yourself in their history, and savor their local cuisines. Here are some recommendations for additional days in some of the popular departure cities for Rhine River cruises:

Basel, Switzerland

Spend extra days in Basel to explore Switzerland's cultural hub. Wander through the Old Town, visit the Basel Minster (cathedral), and enjoy art at the renowned Kunstmuseum Basel. Take a leisurely stroll along the Rhine River promenade, cross the iconic Middle Bridge, and relax at one of the charming cafés.

Amsterdam, Netherlands

Amsterdam offers a wealth of experiences beyond its canals and museums. Take time to explore the Van Gogh Museum, Anne Frank House, and Rijksmuseum. Rent a bike to discover the city like a local, visit the vibrant Jordaan neighborhood, and indulge in Dutch delights at local eateries.

Cologne, Germany

In Cologne, admire the awe-inspiring Cologne Cathedral and explore the historic Old Town. Visit the Chocolate Museum, take a relaxing walk along the Rhine, and try traditional Kölsch beer at a local brewery. Don't miss the opportunity to shop for souvenirs and local products in the city's boutiques and markets.

Strasbourg, France

Extend your stay in Strasbourg to explore its fairytale-like ambiance. Discover the Strasbourg Cathedral and its astronomical clock, explore La Petite France district with its canals and half-timbered houses, and visit the European Parliament. Enjoy a delightful Alsatian dinner at a local restaurant, savoring the region's culinary delights.

Basel, Switzerland (Alternate Departure City)

If you are starting your cruise in Amsterdam or Strasbourg and have the option to depart from Basel, consider arriving a few days early. Basel's museums, galleries, and theaters offer a rich cultural experience, and the city's picturesque surroundings make it an excellent base for day trips to nearby destinations.

By adding extra days in the departure cities, you can extend your travel adventure and make the most of your journey along the Rhine River. Each city has its own unique allure, and exploring them in-depth allows you to create unforgettable memories and discover even more of the diverse cultures and landscapes that make the Rhine River cruise a truly remarkable experience.

Exploring Nearby Regions

A Rhine River cruise is not just a journey along one of Europe's most scenic waterways; it also presents an excellent opportunity to explore nearby regions and expand your travel horizons. Many exciting destinations are easily accessible from the cities and towns along the Rhine River. Here are some nearby regions to consider exploring during your cruise:

Black Forest, Germany
From Strasbourg or Basel, venture into Germany's enchanting Black Forest region. Famous for its dense forests, picturesque villages, and cuckoo clocks, the Black Forest offers opportunities for hiking, cycling, and immersing yourself in traditional German culture. Don't miss sampling the region's delectable Black Forest cake!
Alsace Wine Route, France

From Strasbourg, embark on a journey through the Alsace Wine Route, a scenic route that meanders through charming vineyard-covered landscapes and historic villages. Enjoy wine tastings at family-run wineries, marvel at fairytale castles, and savor the region's renowned Alsatian cuisine.

Romantic Road, Germany

Starting from Basel or Cologne, you can explore the Romantic Road, a scenic route that winds through picturesque Bavarian towns and medieval villages. Experience the quintessential charm of Rothenburg ob der Tauber, visit the fairytale Neuschwanstein Castle, and embrace the magic of Germany's romantic past.

Luxembourg City, Luxembourg

From cities like Strasbourg or Cologne, consider taking a day trip to Luxembourg City, a small but captivating capital known for its UNESCO-listed old town, historic fortifications, and charming casemates. Explore its cultural attractions and enjoy the city's welcoming atmosphere.

Zurich, Switzerland

If you have time before or after your cruise from Basel, consider visiting Zurich, Switzerland's largest city. Discover its vibrant art scene, world-class shopping, and the picturesque shores of Lake Zurich. Take a boat ride, explore the Old Town, and appreciate the stunning views from the Uetliberg Mountain.

Bruges, Belgium

From Amsterdam, consider a trip to Bruges, often referred to as the "Venice of the North." This medieval city is a UNESCO World Heritage Site, boasting well-preserved medieval architecture, cobblestone streets, and scenic canals. Enjoy a boat tour, sample Belgian chocolates, and wander through the charming squares.

Heidelberg, Germany

From Basel or Cologne, venture to Heidelberg, a historic university town known for its romantic castle ruins and the Old Bridge over the Neckar River. Stroll along the Philosopher's Walk for breathtaking views of the city and explore the vibrant student atmosphere.

By exploring nearby regions during your Rhine River cruise, you'll enrich your travel experience and discover the diverse cultural and natural wonders that Europe has to offer. Whether you're drawn to historic towns, scenic landscapes, or culinary delights, these nearby destinations provide an enticing extension to your river cruise adventure.

River Cruise Extensions and Combination Cruises

A Rhine River cruise is just the beginning of your European adventure, and you can further enhance your travel experience with river cruise extensions and combination cruises. These options allow you to explore additional destinations and delve deeper into the cultural richness of the continent. Here are some enticing river cruise extensions and combination cruises to consider:

Danube River Cruise Extension

Extend your river journey by embarking on a Danube River cruise. The Danube, Europe's second-longest river, meanders through multiple countries, including Austria, Hungary, and Romania. Discover the imperial grandeur of Vienna, explore Budapest's majestic landmarks, and experience the enchanting charm of the Wachau Valley. A Danube River cruise provides an opportunity to encounter even more European cultural gems.

Rhine-Moselle Combination Cruise

Combine your Rhine River cruise with a Moselle River cruise to immerse yourself in the beauty of both waterways. Sail through the scenic Moselle

Valley, renowned for its terraced vineyards and charming wine villages. Explore medieval towns like Cochem and Bernkastel-Kues, and savor some of Europe's finest Riesling wines.

Seine River Cruise Extension

Extend your Rhine River cruise with a Seine River cruise in France. Cruise through the heart of Paris, known as the "City of Light," and immerse yourself in the artistic heritage of Monet's Giverny and the historic significance of the Normandy region. A Seine River cruise allows you to delve into France's rich cultural and culinary offerings.

Elbe River Cruise Extension

From Dresden or Berlin, extend your Rhine River cruise with an Elbe River cruise. Journey through picturesque landscapes and historic cities in Germany and the Czech Republic. Explore the stunning sandstone formations of the Saxon Switzerland National Park and visit the beautifully preserved town of Cesky Krumlov.

Mediterranean Cruise Combination

For a more extensive adventure, combine your Rhine River cruise with a Mediterranean cruise. Embark on a journey through the Mediterranean, exploring iconic destinations like Barcelona, Rome, Athens, and Istanbul. Experience the diverse cultures, ancient history, and stunning coastal landscapes of the Mediterranean region.

Tulip Time Cruise Extension

If you're cruising the Rhine during spring, consider a Tulip Time cruise extension in the Netherlands. Sail through the colorful fields of tulips and visit the famous Keukenhof Gardens, a spectacular display of floral beauty. Experience the Netherlands in full bloom and witness its springtime magic.

River cruise extensions and combination cruises offer a seamless way to extend your travels and explore even more of Europe's cultural riches.

FREQUENTLY ASKED QUESTIONS

How Much Should I Budget for a Rhine River Cruise?

Budgeting for a Rhine River cruise involves considering various factors, such as the cruise line, cabin category, travel dates, and additional expenses. While prices can vary, here's a general guide to help you plan your budget for a Rhine River cruise:

Cruise Fare

The cruise fare is the primary cost and varies depending on the cruise line, duration, and cabin type. Standard cabin categories (inside, outside, balcony) typically have different price ranges. Suite accommodations and premium cabin categories come at a higher cost. Prices may range from $1,500 to $5,000 per person for a 7-night Rhine River cruise, depending on factors like the cruise line's reputation and included amenities.

Excursions and Activities

While some cruise lines include basic shore excursions in the cruise fare, additional optional excursions often come at an extra cost. Plan for around $50 to $150 per excursion, depending on the activity and destination.

Travel Insurance

Travel insurance is essential for protecting your investment in case of unforeseen events. Prices for travel insurance can vary based on your age, coverage level, and trip cost, but budget around 5% to 10% of your total trip cost for comprehensive coverage.

Flights and Transportation

If you need to book flights to reach the departure city and return home, budget for airfare. Transportation from the airport to the cruise port may also incur additional costs.

Pre- and Post-Cruise Accommodation

If you plan to arrive a day or two early or stay a few extra days after the cruise to explore the departure or arrival city, budget for additional accommodation expenses.

Gratuities and Onboard Expenses

Many cruise lines include gratuities in the cruise fare, but if it's not included, budget around $10 to $20 per person, per day, for gratuities. Onboard expenses for drinks, specialty dining, spa treatments, and souvenirs should also be considered.

Travel Visas and Documentation

If required, budget for travel visas or other necessary documentation for visiting specific countries along the cruise route.

Personal Expenses

Allocate a budget for personal expenses such as shopping, extra activities, and other incidentals.

Overall, for a 7-night Rhine River cruise, a budget of approximately $2,500 to $6,000 per person (excluding flights) should provide a good range for most travelers. However, it's essential to research specific cruise options, compare prices, and consider any additional preferences or inclusions you may desire. Booking early, taking advantage of promotions, and opting for shoulder season departures may also help you find more budget-friendly options for your dream Rhine River cruise.

CONCLUSION

The Rhine River invites you on a captivating voyage, weaving through Europe's diverse landscapes and unfolding a tapestry of cultural riches along the way. From the enchanting canals of Amsterdam to the timeless beauty of the Cologne Cathedral and the picturesque vineyards of Alsace, the Rhine River cruise promises an unforgettable adventure that will leave you with lasting memories.

Explore historic cities steeped in tradition, indulge in delectable cuisine, and immerse yourself in the art and architecture that define Europe's storied past. Whether you're embarking on a family adventure, a romantic getaway, or a journey of discovery with friends, a Rhine River cruise offers something for everyone.

As the sun sets over the Rhine, painting the sky with hues of gold, you'll find yourself mesmerized by the breathtaking beauty that surrounds you. The charm of each port of call, the warmth of the local communities, and the comfort of your floating sanctuary all blend to create a truly immersive and enriching experience.

Thank you for journeying with us through this Rhine River Cruise. We hope this comprehensive guide has inspired you to set sail along the Rhine, uncovering the enchanting destinations and cultural treasures that await you. Bon voyage and may your Rhine River cruise be filled with moments of wonder and awe!

BONUS

Of course! Whether you're using a smartphone or a digital camera, these 10 photography tips will help you capture stunning shots:

Master Composition: Pay attention to the rule of thirds, leading lines, symmetry, and other compositional techniques. These principles guide the viewer's eye and make your photos more engaging.

Find Good Lighting: Lighting can make or break a photo. Shoot during the golden hours (shortly after sunrise and before sunset) for soft, warm light. Stay away from the intense midday light since it can cast unattractive shadows.

Steady Your Shot: Keep your camera steady to prevent blurry images. Use a tripod, brace your arms against your body, or lean against a stable surface when possible. Many smartphones and cameras also have image stabilization features you can enable.

Focus and depth of field: To bring attention to your subject, use selective focus. On smartphones, tap the screen to focus on your desired point. On cameras, experiment with aperture settings to control depth of field.

Clean the Lens: Fingerprints and dust can degrade image quality. Keep your smartphone or camera lens clean by gently wiping it with a microfiber cloth.

Get Close and Fill the Frame: Eliminate distractions by filling the frame with your subject. This technique creates more impact and draws the viewer's attention directly to the main subject.

Try different perspectives: don't just take pictures at eye level. Try crouching down low or finding a higher vantage point to add a unique perspective to your photos.

Use the Grid and Level: Enable the grid on your smartphone or camera to help align your shots properly. Ensure horizons are straight to avoid distracting tilted landscapes.

Capture Candid Moments: Candid shots often have more genuine emotions. Capture people in their natural state, and if you're taking portraits, try to evoke authentic expressions.

Edit Thoughtfully: Post-processing can enhance your images, but use editing software judiciously. Adjust exposure, contrast, and colors to bring out the best in your photos without going overboard.

Remember, practice makes perfect, so don't be afraid to experiment and learn from both successful and unsuccessful shots. Happy shooting!

Made in the USA
Middletown, DE
17 October 2023

40968138R00073